Pearls *of* Wisdom

THE ULTIMATE COLLECTION OF GREAT QUOTATIONS

ASHOK SAWHNEY

MANJUL

Manjul Publishing House

First published in India by

MANJUL

Manjul Publishing House

• 7/32, Ansari Road, Daryaganj, New Delhi 110 002
Website: www.manjulindia.com

Registered Office:
10, Nishat Colony, Bhopal 462 003 - India

Distribution Centres
Ahmedabad, Bengaluru, Bhopal, Kolkata, Chennai, Hyderabad, Mumbai, New Delhi, Pune

This edition first published in India in 2018

Pearls of Wisdom

ISBN 978-81-8322-650-9

Printed and bound in India by Thomson Press (India) Ltd.

Parents' love is whole, no matter how many times divided.
My parents gave me my life, then they tried to give me their life.
I will never know what sacrifices they went through for me.
I will always appreciate my parents.

My parents-in-law were the ones who loved me unconditionally. We have to earn it from the rest of the world. No matter how far I come, they are always in me.

About the Author

Ashok Sawhney, a leading name in the Indian watch-making industry, has other remarkable qualities apart from entrepreneurship: he is a multilinguist and writes excellent Urdu poetry.

A veteran industrialist, Ashok established his first wrist-watch manufacturing unit in India in 1970, after gaining valuable experience at the Langendorf Watch Company in Switzerland. As a true nationalist, his objective was to reduce dependence on imports. Today, his five watch-making units employ over 2,000 people. Ashok is Global President of Swiss Military, the luxury retail brand from Switzerland, which sells its products in 15 countries worldwide. He was awarded the 'Udyog Patra Samman' by the Institute of Trade and Industrial Development in 2002.

Ashok is fluent in seven languages. His Urdu poetry is highly acclaimed and has found patrons in contemporary Urdu poets and prominent Muslim universities alike. He is the author of **Surbhi Suman**, which is a collection of classic Urdu poetry and **Kya, Kyun, Kaise?** – a compilation of question and answers on commonly observed Indian customs.

He also serves as a Trustee on the board of these renowned institutions:

- Chief Patron of Dr Zakir Hussain Trust, Aligarh
- Trustee of Guru Teg Bahadur International Trust

- ashoksawhney1938@gmail.com
- http://www.grexoft.com/urduhaijiskanaam/Books/surbhisuman
- Ashok Sawhney on YouTube

In Praise of the Book

Ashok Sawhney is a remarkable amalgam of someone in the thick of commerce and business who continues to passionately pursue the finer aesthetics of life. He lives, breathes, talks and absorbs poetry, music and multiple forms of creativity in his unending search for the nobler nuances of life. His eclectic compilation of Urdu and Hindi couplets decades ago, was a great hit and a constant bedside companion for many. Its index unerringly captured the mood, the words and the sense one was looking for in the search for an apposite couplet.

Hence, "**Pearls of Wisdom**" was a logical English corollary and sequel to the aforesaid extremely popular "Surbhi Suman." He has rightly not ignored his English speaking fan following. This book has laughter, wit, pathos, spirituality, anger – in a nutshell, it attempts to capture comprehensively almost all emotions and facets of human existence and to provide solace and support for each with an appropriate quotation, taken from the mouths of our path finders, seers and savants. If Francis Bacon (quoted in the book) was right that "the genius, unity and spirit of a nation are discovered in its proverbs," then Ashok Sawhney has done a great service to our day and age by attempting to encapsulate as much as possible, of such wisdom, in this most handy compilation. It would be invidious to select my favourites but two examples will tell you how much you would enjoy leafing through this labor of love,

Noel Coward – Edna you almost look like a Man.

Novelist Edna – So do you.

Lady Astor – Winston if you were my husband, I would poison your coffee.

Winston Churchill – Madam, if you were my wife, I would drink it.

So go ahead and enjoy an intellectual treat.

Abhishek Singhvi
Member of Parliament,
Spokesperson (INC)

We meet men of letters, eloquent orators, talented poets, patrons of art and culture but it is so rare to find a person possessing all of these qualities. Ashok Sawhney is one such person. He not only combines these qualities but is also a generous and compassionate individual. He is always keen to give away his wealth and time for generous causes. He also shares with readers his wit and wisdom in the form of his books, which in his own words are 'books of the hour and books of all times'. First came "**Khusbu-E-Chaman**" in Urdu which was followed by "**Surbhi Suman**" a compilation of Urdu couplets in Devanagari Script. Many of our queries about topics of life and living were attempted to be answered in his next book **Kya, Kyun, Kaise**. This book was published both in English and Hindi.

These books were followed by his latest book "**Pearls of Wisdom**", a masterly collection of utterances of famous persons and proverbs on topics touching our day to day life. **Pearls of wisdom** and his other books are such that one would wish to keep them on one's bedside as reference books.

Along with other witty quotes are Sawhney's own gems of wisdom interspersed in the book.

I compliment Ashok Sawhney for these books and wish to see more such work from his pen in days to come.

B.L. Joshi
Former Governor of U.P.,
Uttarakhand and Meghalaya

Author's note

We all know that gems of knowledge are "Pearls of Wisdom". These pearls come in the form of quotes, which are the inspirational writings by the world's greatest thinkers. These quotations enlighten our minds and enthuse our hearts. They are the essence of what the wisest men of the world have said and are packed with wisdom and experiences of the ages. This wisdom and experience may be preserved by quotations. Books can be classified broadly into two categories – books of the hour and books of all time. I prefer to write the latter.

I have translated some thoughts from Urdu and Hindi Poetry into English quotes. They can never give the same impression but, you can enjoy the central idea for sure, as reading is a silent conversation.

After a careful study, I have observed that many popular quotes have been retold by other personalities after a lapse of few decades. I'm mentioning some quotes to give you an idea as to who could be the original writer of the same.

We must also remember that, "Originality is the art of remembering what you read somewhere and then forgetting, where you read it."

1. "In prayer it is better to have a heart without words than words without a heart." Mahatma Gandhi (1869-1948) and John Bunyan (1628-1688)
2. "Age is an issue of mind over matter, if you don't mind it doesn't matter". Mark Twain (1835-died), Satchel Paige (1906-1982), Mohammad Ali (1942-2016) and Jack Benny (Born 1982)
3. "An ounce of performance is worth pounds of performances." Mae West (1893-1980)

   "An ounce of action is worth a ton theory." Joe Paterno (1926-2012)

"An ounce of work is worth pounds of preaching." Mahatma Gandhi (1869-1948)

4. "To avoid criticism, do nothing, say nothing and be nothing." Aristotle (1791-1882) and Elbert Hubbard (1856-1915)

5. "The only thing that you take with you when you are gone is what you leave behind." John Aliston (1910-2004) and Avril Lavigne (Born 1984)

6. "Life is not measured by the number of breaths you take but the moments that take your breath away." Phillip James Balley (1816-1902), Denis Waltley (1897-1977), Maya Angelou (1928-2014), George Carlin (1937-2008), Vicky Corona, Hilary Cooper, Kevin Busch (1963-2009), Will Smith (Born 1968)

7. "The way to love anything is to realise that it may be lost." G. K. Chesterton (1874-1936) and Kate Wicker (1887-1958).

8. "Lead, follow or get out of the way." Thomas Paine (1737-1809).

   "Do something. Either lead, follow or get out of the way." Ted Turner (Born 1938)

9. "I have promises to keep, miles to go before I sleep, and miles to go before I sleep." Robert Frost (1874-1963) and Pt. Jawahar Lal Nehru (1889-1964)

10. "There is no exercise better for the heart than reaching down and lifting people up." John Holmes (1944-1988) Dr. Naresh Trehan (Born 1946)

11. "Don't wait, the time will never be just right." Mark Twain (1835-1910) and Napoleon Hill (1883-1970)

12. "Experience is something you don't get until just after you need it." Steven Wright (1955-)

    "Experience is something you get . . . after you need it." Jill Shalvis (Born 1963)

13. "There are basically two types of people, who accomplished

things, and people who claim to have accomplished things. The first group is less crowded." Mark Twain (1835-1910) and Indira Gandhi (1917-1984)

14. "It is long journey, between human beings and being human, think twice." Osho (1931-1990).

    "There is a big difference between human beings and being human." Ratan Tata (born 1937)

15. "All things come to him that waits." Vivekananda (1863-1902) "Everything comes if only a man will wait." Benjamin Disraeli (1804-1881)

16. "I am a man of simple tastes, I am always satisfied with the best." Oscar Wilde (1854-1900)

    "My tastes are simple. I am easily satisfied with the best." Winston Churchill (1874-1965)

17. "Good judgement comes from experience, and a lot of that comes from bad judgement." Rita Mae Brown (born 1944)

    "Good judgement comes from experience and experience comes from bad judgement." Sen Bob Packwood (born 1932)

18. "I do not believe in taking the right decision, I take a decision and make it right." Mohammad Ali Jinnah (1876-1948) and Ratan Tata (Born 1937)

19. "A diplomat is someone who can tell you to go to hell in such a way that you actually look forward to the trip." Caskie Stinnett (1911-1998)

    "Tact is the ability to tell someone to go to hell in such a way that they look forward to the trip." Sir Winston Churchill (1874-1965)

20. "Education is what remains after one has forgotten what one has learnt in school." Albert Einstein (1879-1955)

    "Education is what survives when what has been learnt has been forgotten." B.F. Skinner (1904-1990)

21. "There is nothing on this earth more to be prized than true

friendship." MarkTwain (1835-1910) and Thomas Aquinas (1224-1274)

22. "The most wasted of all days is one without laughter." Nicolas Chamfort (1741-1794), E. E. Cummings (1894-1962) and Charlie Chaplin (1889-1977)

23. "Divide and rule, the politician cries; Unite and lead, is watchword of the wise." Von Goethe (1749-1832).

    "Divide and Rule." Gandhi said about British policy in India.

24. "The best way to predict your future is to create it." Abraham Lincoln (1809-1865) and Peter Drucker. (1909-2005)

    "The only way to predict the future is, to have power to shape the future." Eric Hoffer (1898-1983)

The quotes and the proverbs in this book reflect the experiences of our lives.

To inspire means to infuse with life. Such inspiring quotes by the world's most prominent thinkers, do influence our thinking, arouse us from our dampened spirits, and enliven our sensitivity to the meanings of our very lives. Such motivational ideas and quotes also exalt us by strengthening our hearts and restoring confidence in our souls.

This is the first part of my book **Pearls of Wisdom** and I will continue this effort in future. God bless you all.

—Ashok Sawhney

Contents

1. Achievement *21*
2. Age *25*
3. Aspiration, Inspiration and Imagination *31*
4. Awareness, Ambition, Eyes and Vision *34*
5. Beauty, Elegance and Grace 38
6. Bible, Bhagavad Gita, Vedas and Vedanta 42
7. Body, Heart, Soul and Health 44
8. Character and Habits 49
9. Parents and Children 54
10. Confidence 59
11. Courage, Fear, Strength and Weakness 62
12. Creed, Caste, Conscience and Culture 71
13. Praise, Criticism and Advice 74
14. Determination and Will 78
15. Education and Teacher 80
16. Faith, Religion, Belief and Doubts 84
17. Friends and Foes 91
18. Gifts 102

19. Goodness and Kindness 104

20. Happiness, Sadness, Laughter, Smile and Tears 109

21. Helpfulness and Selfishness 118

22. Home and House 121

23. Hope, Worry and Despair 123

24. Morality, Immortality, Joy and Humanity 126

25. Life and Death 129

26. Love, Hate and Affection 138

27. Nation, India, Ballot and Language 145

28. Nature and Science 148

29. Opportunity, Goal, Variety and Unity 151

30. War and Peace 154

31. World, Universe, Planet and Earth 158

32. Society, Youth, Men, Women and People 162

33. Prayer, Worship and Poetry 174

34. God, Lord and Devil 178

35. Thankfulness and Gratitude 184

36. Yesterday, Today and Tomorrow 186

37. Problems, Troubles and Solutions 189

38. Wisdom and Foolishness 192

39. Work, Action and Practice 197

40. Justice and Punishment 205

41. Knowledge and Ignorance 208

42. Marriage and Divorce 212

43. Revenge and Forgiveness 218

44. Music 221

45. Honesty and Integrity 222

46. Silence, Solitude and Contentment 224

47. Sufferings, Comfort and Pain 228

48. Mind, Ideas and Thoughts 229

49. Sin, Virtue and Spirituality 232

50. Politicans, Diplomacy, King and Government 234

51. Present, Past and Future 237

52. Victory, Defeat, Freedom and Democracy 239

53. Attitude and Simplicity 241

54. Ego, Pride and Humility 246

55. Anger, Frustration and Bad Temper 248

56. Hero, Leader, Genius and Martyr 251

57. Truth and Falsehood 253

58. Time, News and Newspapers 256

59. Success and Failure, Losing and Winning 260

60. Money, Wealth and Price 267

61. Fate, Luck, Fortune and Destiny 270

62. Stress, Strain and Tension 272

63. Miscellaneous 274

64. Rich, Poor, Adversity and Misery 279

65. Experience 282
66. Art and Culture 284
67. Relationships 286
68. Need, Greed and Contentment 289
69. Patience, Light and Darkness 291
70. Charity and Donation 293
71. Wit and Humour 295
72. Global Proverbs 307

1

Achievement

Failed in business in 1831.
Defeated for Legislature in 1832.
Second failure in business in 1833.
Suffered nervous breakdown in 1836.
Defeated for Speaker in 1838.
Defeated for Elector in 1840.
Defeated for Congress in 1843.
Defeated for Senate in 1855.
Defeated for Vice President in 1856.
Defeated for Senate in 1858.
Elected President in 1860.

Lincoln's road to the White House

"Show me a thoroughly satisfied man, and I will show you a failure."
Thomas A. Edison

"The secret of success is consistency of purpose."
Benjamin Disraeli

"Motivation is what gets you started. Habit is what keeps you going."
Jim Rohn

"Do not follow where the path may lead. Go instead where there is no path and leave a trail."

Ralph Waldo Emerson

"The greater the obstacle, the more glory in overcoming it."

Moliere

"I don't agree with – do or die; I say instead – do before you die."

Ashok Sawhney

"First they ignore you, then they laugh at you, then they fight you, then you win."

Mahatma Gandhi

"The greatest danger for most of us is not that our aim is too high and we miss it but that it is too low and we reach it."

Michelangelo

"It doesn't matter where you are coming from. All that matters is where you are going."

Brian Tracy

"The first step to getting the things you want out of life is this: Decide what you want."

Ben Stein

"To climb steep hills requires a slow pace at first."

William Shakespeare

"The three great essentials to achieve anything worthwhile are, first, hard work; second, stick-to-itiveness; third, common sense."

Thomas A. Edison

"Only those who will risk going too far can possibly find out how far one can go."

T. S. Eliot

"You've got to be a little different if you want to get noticed. After all, would anyone give the Tower of Pisa a second glance if it were standing straight?"

Monique Van Vooren

"Definiteness of purpose is the starting point of all achievement."

W. Clement Stone

"The roots of true achievement lie in the will to become the best that you can become."

Harold Taylor

"Desire is the starting point of all achievement, not a hope, not a wish, but a keen pulsating desire which transcends everything."

Napoleon Hill

"Moments erred, centuries suffered."

Ashok Sawhney

"Success has always been easy to measure. It is the distance between one's origins and one's final achievement."

Michael Korda

"Only those who dare to fail greatly can ever achieve greatly."

Robert F. Kennedy

"Only those who attempt the absurd can achieve the impossible."

Albert Einstein

"Even a mistake may turn out to be the one thing necessary to a worthwhile achievement."

Henry Ford

"Never mistake activity for achievement."

John Wooden

"Either write something worth reading or do something worth writing."

Benjamin Franklin

"If you cannot do great things, do small things in a great way."

Napoleon Hill

"It is never too late to be what you might have been."

George Eliot

"First decide your destination. Then do what you have to do."

Ashok Sawhney

2

Age

"Don't regret growing older. It's a privilege denied to many."

Dr. Zuleyka Zevallos

"We don't stop playing because we grow old; we grow old because we stop playing."

George Bernard Shaw

"How old you would be if you did not know how old you were."

Satchel Paige

"When a man is old enough to do wrong he should be old enough to do right also."

Oscar Wilde

"To be seventy years young is sometimes far more cheerful and hopeful than to be forty years old."

Oliver Wendell Holmes

"So long as enthusiasm lasts, so long is youth still with us."

David Starr Jordan

"It is the human bodies that get older and perish but spirits never die, they just change bodies"

Ashok Sawhney

"We are happier in many ways when we are old than when we were young. The young sow wild oats, the old grow sage."

Winston Churchill

"Age is an issue of mind over matter, if you don't mind it doesn't matter."

Mark Twain

"Age does not protect you from love, but love to some extent protects you from age."

Anais Nin

"You are never too old to set another goal or to dream a new dream."

C.S. Lewis

"Being entirely honest with oneself is a good exercise."

Sigmund Freud

"It takes a long time to become young."

Pablo Picasso

"What is the definition of old age – 'when it takes the whole night,' to do once what you once used to do the whole night."

Jeher

"Life would be infinitely happier if we could only be born at the age of eighty and gradually approach eighteen."

Mark Twain

"Love has no age, no limit; and no death."

John Galsworthy

"Age has its own glory, beauty, and wisdom that belong to it."

Joseph Murphy

"Aging has a wonderful beauty and we should have respect for that."

Eartha Kitt

"Beautiful young people are accidents of nature, but beautiful old people are works of art."

Eleanor Roosevelt

"Aging is not lost youth but a new stage of opportunity and strength."

Betty Freidan

"Every age can be enchanting, provided you live within it."

Brigitte Bardot

"Life had engraved such beauty in those lines of age and wisdom."

Rosslyn Elliott

"Maturity is not measured by age. It's an attitude built by experience."

Iarof

"As we grow old, the beauty steals inward."

Ralph Waldo Emerson

"The old believe everything, the middle-aged suspect everything, the young know everything."

Oscar Wilde

"If you keep an active life, you stay young."

Lailah Gifty Akita

"None are so old as those who have outlived enthusiasm."

Henry David Thoreau

"Only a few people grew up in life, the rest just grew old."

Swami Sukhbodhananda

"Be positive to look younger."

Shad Helmsteter

"Older men declare war. But it is youth that must fight and die."

Herbert Hoover

"Age isn't how old you are but how old you feel."

Gabriel Garcia Marquez

"You don't stop laughing because you grow old. You grow old because you stop laughing."

Michael Pritchard

"That's one of the things we learn as we grow older – how to forgive. It comes easier at forty than it did at twenty."

L.M. Montgomery

"One crowded hour of glorious life is worth an age without a name."

Thomas Osbert Mordaunt

"But youth smiles without any reason. It is one of its chiefest charms."

Oscar Wilde

"You start out happy that you have no hips or boobs. All of a sudden you get them, and it feels sloppy. Then just when you start liking them, they start drooping."

Cindy Crawford

"Youth is a disease from which we all recover."

Dorothy Fuldheim

"We were all so young that there were no lines on our faces to read between."

Phyllis Theroux

"About the only thing that comes to us without effort is old age."

Gloria Pitzer

"It's easy to grow old if you haven't grown up."

John Hively

"Age is a cruel monster and time is no friend."

Oluseyi Akinbami

"With age comes wisdom, but sometimes age comes alone."

Oscar Wilde

"Some women wear a miniskirt to reveal their thighs; some wear one to conceal their age."

Mokokoma Mokhonoana

"Be charming at any age."

Lailah Gifty Akita

"A person gets built and stands for a few years and then nature's demolition team comes in."

Dan Groat

"Always educate yourself regardless of how old you are."

Eraldo Banovac

"When the age is in, the wit is out."

William Shakespeare

"One is never too late to become young at heart."

Nadun Lokuliyanage

"Young men think old men fools, old men know young men to be so."

Pravinee Hurbungs

"Courage has no age."

Anne Fortier

"If youth was sold in a bottle of hair dye, we would all get in line."

Jan Rogers

"If a woman tells you she's twenty and looks sixteen, she's twelve. If she tells you she's twenty-six and looks twenty-six, she's damn near forty."

Chris Rock

"Knowledge comes through suffering and wisdom through old age."

Ashok Sawhney

"Knowledge in youth is wisdom in age."

Ziad K. Abdelnour

"A successful man is like a bottle of wine, just gets better with age."

Habeeb Akande

"Prettiness fades after a few years, but elegance only increases with age."

Anne Gracie

"More women grow old nowadays through the faithfulness of their admirers than through anything else."

Oscar Wilde

"Our most important are our earliest years."

William Cowper

"Youth is a blunder, manhood a struggle; old age a regret."

Benjamin Disraeli

3

Aspiration, Inspiration and Imagination

"Learn to let go. That is the key to happiness."

Buddha

"Its easier to fight for one's principles than to live up to them."

Alfred Adler

"It is better to wear out than to rust out."

Bishop Richard Cumberland

"One must forever strive for excellence, or even perfection, in any task however small, and never be satisfied with the second best."

J. R. D. Tata

"Be enthusiastic till it thrills you. Display it, radiate it, till it infects all those around."

Homi Kharas

"Much of the stress that people feel doesn't come from having too much to do. It comes from not finishing what they started."

David Allen

"Life isn't about finding yourself. Life is about creating yourself."

George Bernard Shaw

"You see things; and you say, 'Why?' But I dream things that never were; and I say, 'Why not?"

George Bernard Shaw

"Everything is theoretically impossible, until it is done."

Robert A. Heinlein

"See for the highest, aim at that highest, and you shall reach the highest."

Swami Vivekananda

"There's no shortcut to anywhere worth going."

Thomas Alva Edison

"The important thing is, not to stop questioning."

Albert Einstein

"Take care to get what you like or you will be forced to like what you get."

George Bernard Shaw

"I can teach anybody how to get, what they want out of life. The problem is that I can't find anybody who can tell me what they want."

Mark Twain

"A journey of a thousand miles begins with a single step."

Lao Tzu

"You cannot be lonely if you like the person you're alone with."

Wayne Dyer

"We cannot direct the wind but we can adjust our sails."

Thomas S. Monson

"How I like to be liked, and what I do to be liked!"

Charles Lamb

"The people who get on in this world are the people who get up and look for the circumstances they want and if they can't find them, make them."

George Bernard Shaw

"If you think you're too small to make a difference, try sleeping with a mosquito."

Dalai Lama

"You don't have to see the whole staircase, just take the first step."

Martin Luther King

"My beloved has destroyed me in such a way, that nothing is lost, yet nothing remains."

Ashok Sawhney

4

Awareness, Ambition, Eyes and Vision

"Love is when you meet someone who tells you something new about yourself."

Andre Breton

"The best way to succeed in this world is to act on the advice you give to others."

Mother Teresa

"If a man has not discovered something that he will die for, he isn't fit to live."

Martin Luther King, Jr.

"Nobody remembers who finished second, but the guy who finished second."

Bobby Unser

"You can't wait for inspiration, You have to go after it."

Jack London

"The fire that warms us can also consume us; it is not the fault of the fire."

Swami Vivekananda

"Let us not look back in anger, or forward in fear, but around in awareness."

James Thurber

"Learn everything that is good from others, but bring it in, and in your own way adsorb it; do not become others."

Swami Vivekananda

"Two men look out through the same bars; one sees the mud and one the stars."

Frederick Langridge

"Thousand of candles can be lighted from a single candle and the life of the candle itself will not be shortened."

Gautam Budha

"Some people are grumbling because roses have thorns; I am thankful that thorns have roses."

Alphonse Jean Karr

"I alone cannot change the world, but I can cast a stone across the waters to create many ripples."

Mother Teresa

"It's fine to celebrate success but it is more important to heed the lessons of failure."

Bill Gates

"No one can make you feel inferior without your consent."

Eleanor Roosevelt

"The secret of business is to know something that nobody else knows."

Aristotle Onassis

"Put your hand on a hot stove for a minute, and it seems like an hour. Sit with a pretty girl for an hour, and it seems like a minute. That's relativity."

Albert Einstein

"We must believe that we are gifted for something, and that this thing, at whatever cost, must be attained."

Marie Curie

"A man who views the world the same at fifty as he did at twenty, has wasted thirty years of his life."

Mohammad Ali

"I had the blues because I had no shoes until upon the street, I met a man who had no feet."

Danis Waitley

"The most pathetic person in the world is someone who has sight, but no vision."

Helen Keller

"We are not creatures of circumstances; we are creators of circumstances."

Benjamin Disraeli

"Do not mind anything that anyone tells you about anyone else. Judge everyone and everything for yourself."

Henry James

"Eye contact is more intimate than words will ever be."

Faraaz Kazi

"Be like a tree and let the dead leaves drop."

Jalal ad-Din-Rumi

"We don't meet people by accident. They are meant to cross our path for a reason."

Zig Ziglar

"Ambition is the first step to success. The second step is action."

Evan Carmichael

"The eyes have one language everywhere."

George Hubert

"Eyes can speak and eyes can understand."

George Chapman

"It appears as if you are always with me, when no one else is there."

Ashok Sawhney

5

Beauty, Elegance and Grace

"A beautiful eye makes silence eloquent; a kind eye makes contradiction as assent; an enraged eye makes beauty deformed."

Thomas A. Edison

"Beauty is God's handwriting."

Charles Kingsley

"In every man's heart there is a secret nerve that answers to the vibrations of beauty."

Christopher Morley

"Beauty is worse than wine; it intoxicates both the holder and the beholder."

Aldous Huxley

"As a white candle in a holy place, so is the beauty of an aged face."

Joseph Campbell

"It is amazing how complete is the delusion, that beauty is goodness."

Leo Tolstoy

"The flower which is single, need not envy the thorns that are numerous."

Rabindranath Tagore

"That which is striking and beautiful is not always good; but what is good is always beautiful."

Ninon De L'Enclos

"By plucking her petals you do not gather the beauty of the flower."

Rabindranath Tagore

"It's not what you look at that matters, it's what you see."

Henry David Thoreau

For beautiful eyes, look for the good in others; for beautiful lips, speak only words of kindness; and for poise, walk with the knowledge that you are never alone."

Audrey Hepburn

"To all the girls that think you're fat because you're not a size zero you're the beautiful one, its society who's ugly."

Marilyn Monroe

"Everything has beauty, but not everyone sees it."

Confucius

"Beauty is bought by judgment of the eye."

William Shakespeare

"Some people, no matter how old they get, never lose their beauty - they merely move it from faces into their hearts . . . ."

Martin Buxbaum

"Your outer beauty will capture the eyes, your inner beauty will capture the heart."

Steven Aitchison

"The beauty of the soul grows with age."

Antonio Perez

"Beauty has a lot to do with character."

Kevyn Aucoin

"The world's biggest power is the youth and beauty of a woman."

Chanakya

"A beautiful face is a silent commendation."

Francis Bacon

"A women's greatest asset is her beauty."

Alex Comfort

"Elegance is not about being noticed, it's about being remembered."

Giorgio Armani

"Grace in women has more effect than beauty."

William Hazlitt

"A thing of beauty is a joy forever."

John Keats

"Beauty is in the heart of the beholder."

H. G. Wells

"The benefits of the youth is strength and beauty, the benefit of an old age is the reason."

Democritus

"Beautiful things don't ask for attention."

James Thurber

"Beauty has no relation to price, rarity, or age."

John Cotton

"Beauty is not in the face, beauty is a light in the heart."

Khalil Gibran

"Beauty dwells in purity. Beauty shines in virtues."

Shivanand

"True simplicity is the secret of true beauty."

Sadhu Vaswani

"'Beauty is truth, truth beauty' – that is all ye know on earth, and all ye need to know."

John Keats

"That is the best part of beauty, which a picture cannot express."

Francis Bacon

"Beauty provoketh thieves sooner than gold."

William Shakespeare

6

Bible, Bhagavad Gita, Vedas and Vedanta

"The Gita is the greatest gospel of spiritual works ever yet given to the race."

Sri Aurobindo Ghosh

"What you bring away from the Bible depends to some extent on what you carry to it."

Oliver Wendell Holmes

"No man ever believes that the Bible means what it says: He is always convinced that it says what he means."

George Bernard Shaw

"Give God your weakness and He'll give you His strength."

The Bible

"With man it is impossible, but not with God; all things are possible with God."

The Bible

"Don't worry about everything around you. That's my job."

The Bible

"God answers in 3 ways:
He says yes and gives you what you want.
He says no and gives you something better.
He says wait and gives you the best."

The Bible

"My unknown future is in the hands of the all-knowing God."

The Bible

"In the history of the world, the Vedas fill a gap which no literary work in any other language could fill."

Max Muller

"Saint's life is one long prayer."

Shivanand

"Who builds a church within his heart and takes it with him everywhere is holier far than he whose church is but a one-day house of prayer."

Morris Abel Beer

"Earth has no sorrow that Heaven cannot heal."

Thomas Moore

"None can reach heaven who has not passed through hell."

Shri Arvind

"Go to heaven for the climate, hell for the company."

Mark Twain

"Trees are the earth's endless effort to speak to the listening heaven."

Rabindranath Tagore

"I like the silent church before the service begins, better than any preaching."

Ralph Waldo Emerson

7

Body, Heart, Soul and Health

"To give pleasure to a single heart by a single act is better than a thousand heads bowing in prayer."

Mahatma Gandhi

"Be faithful to that which exists within yourself."

André Gide

"Feeling depressed, is our inner self asking us to listen."

Carolyn Hobbs

"Never look down on anybody unless you're helping them up."

Jesse Jackson

"You have to grow from the inside out. None can teach you, none can make you spiritual. There is no other teacher but your own soul."

Swami Vivekananda

"And a thousand million lives are his,
who carries the world in his sympathies."

James Russell Lowell

"Mirth cannot move a soul in agony."

William Shakespeare

"Learn the approach to art of living from a budding flower, despite the struggle to blossom its aroma never grows faint."

Ashok Sawhney

"No one can be wrong with man and right with God."

Harry Emerson Fosdick

"It's easy to fool the eye, but its hard to fool the heart."

Al Pacino

"The soul in man is greater than his fate."

Shri Arvind

"We are all dependent on one another, every soul of us on earth."

George Bernard Shaw

"As a countenance made beautiful by the soul's shining through it, so the world is beautiful by the shining through it of God."

Friedrich Heinrich Jacobi

"Heaven's call is rare, rarer the heart that heeds."

Shri Arvind

"Unlike a drop of water which loses its identity when it joins the ocean, man does not lose his being in the society in which he lives. Man's life is independent. He is born not for the development of society alone, but for the development of his self."

B R Ambedkar

"Soulmates don't finally meet somewhere. They're in each other all along."

Jalal ad-Din Rumi

"A broken heart is a very pleasant complaint for a man in London, if he has a comfortable income."

George Bernard Shaw

"Ordinary riches can be stolen, real riches cannot. In your soul are infinitely precious things that cannot be taken from you."

Oscar Wilde

"When hearts love they understand each other without any words."

Rabindranath Tagore

"The heart wants what it wants. There's no logic to those things."

Woody Allen

"Not only must we be good, but we must also be good for something."

Henry David Thoreau

"Don't compromise yourself. You are all you've got."

Janis Joplin

"People judge you by your actions, not your intentions, you may have a heart of gold, but so does a hard boiled egg."

Maya Angelou

"No beauty shines brighter than that of a good heart."

Khalil Gibran

"The heart is the only broken instrument that works."

T. E. Kalem

"To handle yourself, use your head; to handle others, use your heart."

Donald laird

"A good conscience is to the soul, what health is to the body."

Thomas A. Edison

"Live within: be not shaken by outward happenings."

Sri Aurobindo Ghosh

"It is health that is real wealth and not pieces of gold and silver."

Mahatma Gandhi

"One learns people through the heart, not the eyes or the intellect."

Mark Twain

"There is no charm equal to tenderness of heart."

Jane Austen

"Happiness resides not in possessions, and not in gold, happiness dwells in the soul."

Democritus

"The best and most beautiful things in the world cannot be seen or even touched - they must be felt with the heart."

Helen Keller

"What the mind can conceive and believe, and the heart desire, you can achieve."

Norman Vincent Peale

"It is chance that makes brothers but heart that make friends."

Von Geibel

"Greed is the heart's greatest enemy."

Dr. Naresh Trehan

"My strength is as the strength of ten; because my heart is pure."

Alfred Lord Tennyson

"If we always find mud around us, it proves that there is mud somewhere in us."

Mother Teresa

"What lies behind us and what lies ahead of us are tiny matters compared to what lies within us."

Ralph Waldo Emerson

"The heart of a fool is in his mouth but the mouth of a wise man is in his heart."

Benjamin Franklin

"The soul is born old but grows young. That is the comedy of life. And the body is born young and grows old. That is life's tragedy."

Oscar Wilde

"A healthy body is the guest chamber of the soul; a sick, its prison."

Francis Bacon

8

Character and Habits

"The measure of a man's real character is what he would do if he knew he would never be found out."

Thomas Macaulay

"How soon 'not now' becomes 'never'."

Martin Luther

"Weakness of attitude becomes weakness of character."

Albert Einstein

"Ability may get you to the top, but it takes character to keep you there."

John Wooden

"Trifles make perfection, and perfection is no trifle."

Michelangelo

"The true perfection of man lies, not in what man has, but in what man is."

Oscar Wilde

"No one is perfect – that's why pencils have erasers."

Wolfgang Riebe

"The Farther a man knows himself to be from perfection, the nearer he is to it."

Gerard Groote

"To love oneself is the beginning of a life-long romance."

Oscar Wilde

"When we have not what we like, we must like, what we have."

Political Ideology

"Keep a secret, it is your slave, tell it and it is your master."

Wilson Allen

"Correct yourself first and all else will become corrected or corrigible."

Ram Tirtha

"Try not to become a person of success, but rather try to become a person of value."

Albert Einstein

"Selfishness is not living as one wishes to live, it is asking others to live as one wishes to live."

Oscar Wilde

"To utter pleasant words without practicing them, is like a fine flower without fragrance."

Gautama Buddha

"Champions aren't made in the gym. Champions are made from something they have deep inside them."

Muhammad Ali

"When a man wants to murder a tiger he calls it sport; when a tiger wants to murder him he calls it ferocity."

George Bernard Shaw

"Sports and power do not build character, it reveals it."

John Wooden

"Men may change their climate but they cannot change their nature."

Joseph Addison

"Whatever you think, that you will be. If you think yourselves weak, weak you will be; if you think yourselves strong, strong you will be."

Swami Vivekananda

"I must complain the cards are ill shuffled, till I have a good hand."

Jonathan Swift

"A signature always reveals a man's character - and sometimes even his name."

Evan Esar

"Eat your food like your medicines, else you will eat medicines as your food."

Amatellah

"The butterfly counts not months but moments, and has time enough."

Rabindranath Tagore

"A person who is nice to you but not nice to the waiter, is not a nice person."

William H. Swanson

"A friend is one who knows you, but loves you anyway."

Jerome Cummings

"Character cannot be developed in ease and quiet. Only through experience of trial and suffering can the soul be strengthened, ambition inspired, and success achieved."

Helen Keller

"If you're walking down the right path and you're willing to keep walking, eventually you'll make progress."

Barack Obama

"The most valuable of all talents is, that of never using two words, when one will do."

Thomas Jefferson

"We are what we repeatedly do. Excellence, then, is not an act, but a habit."

Aristotle

"If you want to test a man's character, give him power."

Abraham Lincoln

"It is better to die on your feet than to live on your knees."

E-Zapata

"The price of greatness is responsibility."

Winston Churchill

"You are a master of every word that you are yet to utter but a slave to every word you have already uttered."

Nithya Shanti

"Never judge someone by the opinion of others."

Zig Ziglar

"I can resist everything except temptation."

Oscar Wilde

"Thoughts are the bricks with which character is built. Character is not born, it is formed."

Shivanand

"Character is like a tree, and reputation is its shadow. The shadow is what we think of it; the tree is the real thing."

Abraham Lincoln

"A mistake repeated more than once is a decision."

Paulo Coelho

"Raise your words, not voice. It is rain that grows flowers, not thunder."

Rumi

"Be the type of person you want to meet."

Dutchess Roz

"If your son is a devil, don't spoil him more with your wealth, if he is an angel, he doesn't need your wealth."

Ashok Sawhney

9

Parents and Children

"Most of all the other beautiful things in life come by twos and threes, by dozens and hundreds. Plenty of roses, stars, sunsets, rainbows, brothers and sisters, aunts and cousins, but only one mother in the whole world."

Kate Douglas Wiggin

"Every child comes with the message that God is not yet discouraged of man."

Rabindranath Tagore

"The mother's heart is the child's school room."

Henery Ward Beecher

"Children are the anchors that hold a mother to life."

Sophocles

"What gift has providence bestowed on man that is so dear to him as his children?"

Cicero

"One father is more than a hundred uncles."

Ashok Sawhney

"Children begin by loving their parents. After a time they judge them. Rarely, if ever, do they forgive them."

Oscar Wilde

"What a child doesn't receive he can seldom later give."

P. D. James

"Don't worry that children never listen to you;
worry that they are always watching you."

Robert Fulghum

"The only way we can ever teach a child to say 'I am sorry' is for him to hear it from our lips first."

Kevin Leman

"Two of the greatest gifts we can give our children are roots and wings."

Hodding Carter

"The only wealth in this world is children. More than all the money, power on the earth."

Michael Corleone

"Ever told your child, we'll do it tomorrow? And in your haste, not see his sorrow?"

David L. Wetherford

"It is easier for a father to have children than for children to have a real father."

Pope John

"Making the decision to have a child is to decide forever to have your heart go walking outside your body."

Elizabeth Stone

"It is not what you leave for your children, but what you taught them, that will make them good human beings."

Ashok Sawhney

"All that I am, or hope to be, I owe to my angel mother."

Abraham Lincoln

"The hand that rocks the cradle is the hand that rules the world."

William Ross Wallace

"Parents wonder why the streams are bitter, when they themselves have poisoned the fountain."

John Locke

"No religion for you, my children, but morality and bravery."

Swami Vivekananda

"Mothers are fonder than fathers of their children because they are more certain that they are their own."

Aristotle

"My father always used to say,
'Don't raise your voice. Improve your argument.'"

Desmond Tutu

"A baby is God's opinion that life should go on."

Carl Sandburg

"Let us sacrifice our today so that our children can have a better tomorrow."

A.P.J. Abdul Kalam

"The first half of our lives is ruined by our parents and the second half by our children."

Clarence Darrow

"The reason grandparents and grandchildren get along so well is that they have a common enemy."

Sam Levenson

"Each day of our lives, we make deposits in the memory banks of our children."

Charles R. Swindoll

"How sharper than a serpent's tooth it is, to have a thankless child."

William Shakespeare

"Never have children, only have grandchildren."

Gore Vidal

"Human beings are the only creatures that allow their children to come back home."

Bill Cosby

"You are the bows from which your children as living arrows are sent forth."

Kahlil Gibran

"Mould your children and you mould the nation."

Shivanand

"Every baby born into the world is a finer one than the last."

Charles Dickens

"Curiosity in children is but an appetite for knowledge."

John Locke

"I don't know who my grandfather was; I am much more concerned to know what his grandson will be?"

Abraham Lincoln

"Live life in a way that when your children think of forgiveness, hardwork, love, care, devotion and integrity - they think of you."

Ashok Sawhney

10

Confidence

"Why should we worry about what others think of us, do we have more confidence in their opinions than we do our own?"

Brigham Young

"People who want the most approval get the least and the people who need approval the least get the most."

Wayne Dyer

"The question isn't who is going to let me; it's who is going to stop me."

Ayn Rand

"I am not a product of my circumstances. I am a product of my decisions."

Stephen Covey

"Define Trust... giving someone the authority to destroy you completely, but having the confidence he would never do it."

Nabil

"Confidence says, 'I can do it!' Faith says, 'Consider it's done!'"

Matthew

"Nothing is impossible, if you believe in yourself."

Swami Vivekananda

"Self-confidence - the foundation of all great success and achievement."

Verica M Tackeon

"Confidence never comes from having all the answers. It comes from being open to all the questions."

Earl Gray Stevens

"He who undervalues himself is justly undervalued by others."

William Hazlitt

"What people say you cannot do, you try and find that you can."

Henry David Thoreau

"Believe you can and you're halfway there."

Theodore Roosevelt

"The most beautiful thing you can wear is confidence."

Blake Lively

"If we all did the things we are capable of doing, we would literally astound ourselves."

Thomas A. Edison

"It is not the mountain we conquer, but ourselves."

Sir Edmund Hillary

"As soon as you trust yourself, you will know how to live."

Johann Wolfgang von Goethe

"I do not believe in taking the right decision, I take a decision and make it right."

Muhammad Ali Jinnah

"No matter what a woman looks like, if she's confident, she's sexy."

Paris Hilton

"All power is within you; you can do anything and everything."

Swami Vivekananda

"Don't be afraid to take a big step, you can't cross chasm in two small jumps."

David Floyd George

"Confidence is like a dragon where, for every head cut off, two more heads grow back."

Criss Jami

"Self-confidence is contagious."

Stephen Richard

"Although I am a confident and strong willed person, yet many a time I need someone to hold my hand and say,'don't worry all will be well.'"

Ashok Sawhney

11

Courage, Fear, Strength and Weakness

"Courage isn't having the strength to go on – it is going on when you don't have the strength."

Napoleon Bonaparte

"Courage is the first of human qualities because it is the quality which guarantees all the others."

Winston Churchill

"In this world there is always danger for those who are afraid of it."

George Bernard Shaw

"Strength of numbers is the delight of the timid. The valiant in spirit glory in fighting alone."

Mahatma Gandhi

"The greater the power, the more dangerous the abuse."

Edmund Burke

"Keep your fears to yourself, but share your courage with others."

Robert Louis Stevenson

"Face the situation fearlessly and soon there will be no situation to face."

Pope John Paul

"It is not the weathercock that changes; it is the wind."

C. Desmoulins

"It's important that people know what you stand for. It's equally important that they know what you won't stand for."

Mary Waldrip

"The strongest man in the world is he who stands most alone."

Henrik Ibsen

"Take risks in your life. If you win, you can lead, if you lose, you can guide."

Swami Vivekananda

"Love is always creative, fear always destructive."

Emmet Fox

"There are terrible temptations that it requires strength, strength and courage, to yield to."

Oscar Wilde

"Necessity makes even the timid brave."

Sallust

"The hero is no braver than an ordinary man, but he is brave five minutes longer."

Ralph Waldo Emerson

"The brave meet death with a smile on their lips."

Mahatma Gandhi

"Nothing is more despicable than respect based on fear."

Albert Camus

"Of all the liars in the world, sometimes the worst are your own fears."

Rudyard Kipling

"When the going gets tough, the tough get going."

Joseph Kennedy

"You will never be anything in the world without courage. It is the greatest quality of the mind - next to honour."

J. L. Allen

"The world is the great gymnasium where we come to make ourselves strong."

Swami Vivekananda

"Have the courage to make mistakes – and learn from them."

Dr. A. S. Raman

"Face the brutes. That is a lesson for all life – face the terrible, face it boldly. Like the monkeys, the hardships of life fall back when we cease to flee before them."

Swami Vivekananda

"Take time to deliberate; but when the time for action arrives, stop thinking and go in."

Napoleon Bonaparte

"Don't let the fear of losing be greater than the excitement of winning."

Robert Kiyosaki

"Love conquers all fears."

Swami Vivekananda

"If you are not willing to risk the usual, you will have to settle for the ordinary."

Jim Rohn

"Success is not final, failure is not fatal: it is the courage to continue that counts."

Winston Churchill

"Fear: False Evidence Appearing Real."

Art Martin Ph.D

"In skating over thin ice, our safety is in our speed."

Ralph Waldo Emerson

"Inaction breeds doubt and fear. Action breeds confidence and courage. If you want to conquer fear, do not sit home and think about it. Go out and get busy."

Dale Carnegie

"The enemy is fear. We think it is hate; but, it is fear".

Mahatma Gandhi

"All our dreams can come true, if we have the courage to pursue them."

Walt Disney

"Courage is resistance to fear, mastery of fear, not absence of fear."

Mark Twain

"The question in life is not whether you get knocked down. You will. The question is, are you ready to get up and fight for what you believe in."

Dan Quayle

"Being deeply loved by someone gives you strength, while loving someone deeply gives you courage."

Lao Tzu

"Union may be strength, but it is mere blind brute strength unless wisely directed."

Samuel Butler

"Where there is no struggle, there is no strength."

Oprah Winfrey

"Never be weak, you must be strong; you have infinite strength within you."

Swami Vivekananda

"It is not because things are difficult that we do not dare, it is because we do not dare that things are difficult."

Seneca

"Never yield to force; never yield to the apparently overwhelming might of the enemy."

Winston Churchill

"The power of the waterfall is nothing but a lot of drops working together"

K B S Logistics

"Anything that makes you weak physically, intellectually and spiritually, reject as poison."

Swami Vivekananda

"He who shows his strength, confirms his weakness."

Rabindranath Tagore

"Strength does not come from physical capacity. It comes from an indomitable will."

Mahatma Gandhi

"F.E.A.R. has two meanings –
Forget everything and run, or face everything and rise. The choice is yours."

Zig Ziglar

"It is curious that physical courage should be so common in the world and moral courage so rare."

Mark Twain

"The weak can never forgive. Forgiveness is the attribute of the strong."

Mahatma Gandhi

"It's not the size of the dog in the fight, it's the size of the fight in the dog."

Mark Twain

"Rudeness is the weak man's imitation of strength."

Eric Hoffer

"God gives his toughest battles to his strongest soldiers."

K. Kehlani

"Our greatest weakness lies in giving up. The most certain way to succeed is always to try just one more time."

Thomas A. Edison

"With the new day comes new strength and new thoughts."

Eleanor Roosevelt

"Great works are performed not by strength but by perseverance."

Samuel Johnson

"You can never cross the ocean until you have the courage to lose sight of the shore."

Christopher Columbus

"It is better to be feared than loved, if you cannot be both."

Niccolo Machiavelli

"The only thing we have to fear is fear itself."

Franklin D. Roosevelt

"Life is either a daring adventure or nothing at all."

Helen Keller

"A ship in the harbour is safe, but that is not what ships are built for."

William Shedd

"Fear is the thought of admitted inferiority."

Elbert Hubbard

"Never forget that only dead fish swim with the stream."

Malcolm Muggeridge

"Never give in, never give in, never, never, never, never, never - in nothing, great or small, large or petty - never give in except to convictions of honour and good sense."

Winston Churchill

"Where there is no struggle, there is no strength."

Oprah Winfrey

"Being both soft and strong is a combination very few have mastered."

Yasmin Mogahed

"Fear of death increases in exact proportion to increase in wealth."

Ernest Hemingway

"Look towards the sun and the shadow will follow you. Look away from the sun and you will have to follow the shadow."

Swamy Ram Tirathi

"Meditation is just a courage to be silent and alone."

Osho

"It requires more courage to suffer than to die."

Napoleon Bonaparte

"Courage is the commitment to begin, without any guarantee of success."

Johann Wolfgang Von Goethe

"The one who falls and gets up is so much stronger than the one who never fell."

Roy T. Bennet

"You're allowed to scream, you're allowed to cry, but do not give up."

Gideon Calvin

"Always go with the choice that scares you the most, because that's the one that is going to help you grow."

Caroline Myss

"Courage is the thing. All goes if courage goes."

James M. Barrie

"The first step to getting what you want is having the courage to get rid of what you don't."

Zig Ziglar

"You don't have to control your thoughts. You just have to stop letting them control you."

Dan Millman

"There are only two forces which unite men; fear and interest."

Napoleon Bonaparte

"Wisdom is learning to let go when you want to hang on.
Courage is learning to hang on when you want to let go."

Mark Amend

"Fear defeats more people than any other one thing in the world."

Ralph Waldo Emerson

12

Creed, Caste, Conscience and Culture

"Modesty is the conscience of the body."

Honore De Balzac

"True culture is the discipline of head, heart and hand."

Shivanand

"Culture opens the sense of beauty."

Ralph Waldo Emerson

"A good conscience is a continual feast."

Francis Bacon

"You aren't wealthy until you have something money can't buy."

Garth Brooks

"War is so unjust and ugly that all who wage it must try to stifle the voice of conscience within themselves."

Leo Tolstoy

"As civilization advances, poetry almost necessarily declines."

Lord Macaulay

"A cheerful, intelligent face is the end of culture."

Ralph Waldo Emerson

"Once a British asked me why can't I wear proper clothes to look like a gentleman. I smiled and said: in your culture, a tailor makes a gentleman; but, in our culture, character makes a gentleman."

Swami Vivekananda

"There is a higher court than courts of justice and that is the court of conscience. It supercedes all other courts."

Mahatma Gandhi

"All tyranny needs to gain a foothold is, for people of good conscience to remain silent."

Edmund Burke

"In looking for people to hire, you look for three qualities: integrity, intelligence and energy. And if they don't have the first, the other two will kill you."

Warren Buffett

"What more can be added to the happiness of a man who is in health, out of debt and has clear conscience."

Adam Smith

"Where there is no law, conscience rules."

Pablilius Cyrus

"Conscience is 'God' for everyone."

Mainander

"Conscience is our individual matter, where majority has no place."

Napolean Bonaparte

"A good conscience is to the soul what health is to the body."

Joseph Addison

"A good digestion depends upon a good conscience."

Benjamin Disraeli

"Conscience is the court room where the good or the bad deeds are continuously judged."

Ashok Sawhney

13

Praise, Criticism and Advice

"An injury is much sooner forgotten than an insult."

Lord Chesterfield

"He who cannot forgive breaks the bridge over which he himself must pass."

George Herbert

"I will praise any man that will praise me."

Shakespeare

"Praise undeserved is scandal in disguise."

Alexander Pope

"He has the right to criticize who has the heart to help."

Abraham Lincoln

"How seldom we weigh our neighbor, in the same balance with ourselves."

Thomas A. Kempis

"Encouragement after censure is as the sun after a shower."

Goethe

"It is amazing what you can accomplish if you do not care who gets the credit."

Harry S. Truman

"We always like those who admire us; we do not always like those whom we admire."

La Rochefoucauld

"Whenever one has anything unpleasant to say, one should always be quite candid."

Oscar Wilde

"The trouble with most of us is that we would rather be ruined by praise than saved with criticism."

Norman Vincent Peale

"We can improve our relationships with others by leaps and bounds if we become encouragers instead of critics."

Joyce Meyer

"The greatest compliment that was ever paid to me was when someone asked me what I thought, and attended to my answer."

Henry David Thoreau

"Criticism is an indirect form of self-boasting."

Emmet Fox

"When virtues are pointed out first, flaws seem less insurmountable."

Judith Martin

"Criticize by creation, not by finding fault."

Marcus Tullius Cicero

"Let me never fall into the vulgar mistake of dreaming that I am persecuted whenever I am contradicted."

Ralph Waldo Emerson

"Don't criticize what you don't understand, son. You never walked in that man's shoes."

Elvis Presley

"Before you go and criticize the younger generation, just remember who raised them."

Antoine De Saint

"Criticism may not be agreeable, but it is necessary. It fulfills the same function as pain in the human body. It calls attention to an unhealthy state of things."

Winston Churchill

"One mustn't criticize other people on grounds where he can't stand perpendicular himself."

Mark Twain

"Don't criticize them; they are just what we would be under similar circumstances."

Abraham Lincoln

"Who sees all beings in his own self, and his own self in all beings, loses all fear."

Isa Upanishad, Hindu Scripture

"Where no hope is left, is left no fear."

John Milton

"Avoiding danger is no safer in the long run than outright exposure. The fearful are caught as often as the bold."

Helen Keller

"Remain even-minded at all times even amidst profit or loss, pleasure or pain, sickness or health, victory or defeat, praise or criticism."

Bhagavad Gita

"If you want to sacrifice the admiration of many men, for the criticism of one, go ahead, get married."

Katharine Hepburn

"If you get your head above the crowd, you are going to be criticized."

Dale Carnegie

"People ask you for criticism but they only want praise."

W. Somerset Maugham

"It is infinitely easier to criticize than to create."

J. McCormick

"Animals are such agreeable friends – they ask no questions, they pass no criticism."

George Eliot

"Unsolicited advice is the cheapest commodity you can find because the supply is so great and the demand so little."

Richard Nixon

"We despise no source that can pay us a pleasing attention."

Mark Twain

"Flatterers look like friends as wolves like dogs."

George Chapman

"There is nothing which we receive with so much reluctance as advice."

Joseph Addison

14

Determination and Will

"O Lord, Thou givest us everything, at the price of an effort."

Leonardo Da Vinci

"And remember, no matter where you go, there you are."

Confucius

"You've got to get up every morning with determination, if you're going to go to bed with satisfaction."

George Lorimer

"You have to learn the rules of the game. And then you have to play better than anyone else."

Albert Einstein

"People do not lack strength, they lack will."

Victor Hugo

"A university should be a place of light, of liberty, and of learning."

Benjamin Disraeli

"Act as if what you do, makes a difference. It does."

William James

"Strength does not come from physical capacity. It comes from an indomitable will."

Mahatma Gandhi

"We can do anything we want to, if we stick to it long enough."

Helen keller

"Whether you think you can or you think you can't, you're right."

Henry Ford

"Nothing is impossible. The word itself says 'I'm possible.'"

Audrey Hepburn

"It's not whether you get knocked down, it's whether you get up."

Vince Lombardi

"Standing in the middle of the road is very dangerous; you get knocked down by the traffic from both sides."

Margaret Thatcher

"What's meant to be will always find a way."

John Lennon

15

Education and Teacher

"If you have knowledge, let others light their candles at it."

Thomas Fuller

"The great difficulty in education is to get experience out of ideas."

George Santayana

"Don't educate your children to be rich. Educate them to be happy. So when they grow up they will know the value of things, not the price."

Ratan Tata

"Qualities of a student – first religious and moral principles; secondly gentlemanly conduct; thirdly, intellectual ability."

Thomas Arnold

"Wear your learning like your pocket watch, in a private pocket; and do not merely pull it out and strike it, merely to show that you have one."

Lord Chesterfield

"Learning teacheth more in one year than experience in twenty."

Roger Ascham

"Educating the mind without educating the heart is no education at all."

Aristotle

"The secret of education lies in respecting the pupil."

Ralph Waldo Emerson

"National education, the surest and most profitable national investment, is as necessary for national safety as the military provision for physical defence."

Lala Lajpat Rai

"We must have teachers who could develop teaching scholars. These teachers must have backing, prestige and a good salary, so that they can attract intellectuals to this noble profession."

Ashok Sawhney

"What sculpture is to a block of marble, education is to the human soul."

Joseph Addison

"The roots of education are bitter, but the fruit is sweet."

Aristotle

"Education costs money. But then so does ignorance."

Sir Claus Moser

"He who can, does. He who cannot, teaches.

George Bernard Shaw

"Education is the key to unlock the golden door of freedom."

George Washington Carver

"The only thing that interferes with my learning is my education."

Albert Einstein

"Education is an admirable thing, but it is well to remember from time to time that nothing that is worth knowing can be taught."

Oscar Wilde

"Teaching is the profession that teaches all other professions."

Preetha D'souza

"I cannot teach anybody anything, I can only make them think."

Socrates

"Learning without thought is labor lost; thought without learning is perilous."

Confucius

"Education is not received. It is achieved."

Albert Einstein

"If we want to reach real peace in this world, we should start educating children."

Mahatma Gandhi

"The man who does not read has no advantage over the man who cannot read."

Mark Twain

"In examinations the foolish ask questions that the wise cannot answer."

Oscar Wilde

"We must be silent before we can listen.
We must listen before we can learn.
We must learn before we can prepare.
We must prepare before we can serve.
We must serve before we can lead."

William Arthur Ward

"Success is a lousy teacher. It seduces smart people into thinking they can't lose."

Bill Gates

"Education is to business what fertilizer is to farming."

Pramod Batra

"It is easier to preach twenty people than to be one of the twenty in following the preaching."

Swami Shivanand

"Live as if you were to die tomorrow; learn as if you were to live forever."

Mahatma Gandhi

"Never stop educating yourself, regardless of your age."

Ashok Sawhney

16

Faith, Religion, Belief and Doubts

"Accept a thing and believe in a religion on its own merits. Examine it yourself. Sift it. Sell not your liberty to Buddha, Jesus, Mohammed, or Krishna."

Swami Ramtirtha

"For those who believe, no proof is necessary, for those who don't believe, no proof is possible."

Stuart Chase

"Non-violence requires a double faith, faith in God and also faith in man."

Mahatma Gandhi

"My faith is that the progress of Islam does not depend on the use of sword by its believers, but the result of the supreme sacrifice of Hussain the great saint."

Mahatma Gandhi

"That which we call the Hindu religion is really the eternal religion because it embraces all others."

Aurobindo Ghosh

"Love is the foundation of all religions."

Rabindranath Tagore

"Religion is not a particular way of life but is the way of all life."

Dr. S. Radhakrishanan

"The true religion is built upon the rock; the rest are tossed upon the waves of time."

Francis Bacon

"Faith is not belief without proof, but trust without reservations."

Elton Trueblood

"One religion is as true as another."

Robert Burton

"Religion, philosophy and meditation must go hand in hand."

Shivanand

"The moment we want to believe something, we suddenly see all the arguments for it, and become blind to the arguments against it."

George Bernard Shaw

"Atheism is rather in the life than in the heart of man."

Francis Bacon

"Religion was his life and life was religion."

Richard Stafford Cripps (on Gandhi Ji)

"I do not want merely to possess a faith; I want a faith that possesses me."

Charles Kingsley

"It is the test of a good religion whether you can joke about it."

G.K. Chesterton

The Rose

"If you doubt there is a God, look deep into a rose;
See the velvet petals from the folded bud unclose;
Note the tint and texture and the lovely coloring;
Could blind Nature of itself evolve so fair a thing?
Feel the softness of the petal, breathe the fragrant scent;
Need you waste another thought on further argument?
Here is proof of a Creator: God made manifest;
In this little rose we see divinity expressed."

Patience Strong

"A small body of determined spirits fired by an unquenchable faith in their mission can alter the course of history."

Mahatma Gandhi

"The fact that a believer is happier than a skeptic is no more to the point than the fact that a drunken man is happier than a sober one."

George Bernard Shaw

"Fear can keep us up all night long, but faith makes one fine pillow."

Philip Gulley

"Religion is the manifestation of the natural strength that is in man."

Swami Vivekananda

"Doubt is an element of criticism."

Benjamin Disraeli

"Ignorance is the mother of suspicion."

William Rounseville Alger

"Suspicion is the poison of true friendship."

St. Augustine

"If a man will begin with certainties, he shall end in doubt but if he will be content to begin with doubts, he shall end in certainties."

Francis Bacon

"There is only one religion, though there are a hundred versions of it."

George Bernard Shaw

"Religion should be our steering wheel, not our spare tyre."

Charles L. Wheeler

"We have just enough religion to make us hate one another but not enough to make us love one another."

Jonathan Swift

"There are no tricks in plain and simple faith."

Shakespeare

"Man prefers to believe what he prefers to be true."

Francis Bacon

"It is easier to believe than to doubt."

Everett D. Martin

"They can conquer who believe they can."

Ralph Waldo Emerson

"Our doubts are traitors, and make us lose the good we oft might win, by fearing to attempt."

Shakespeare

"Human knowledge is the parent of doubt."

Sir Fulke Greville

"Doubt comes in at the window when inquiry is denied at the door."

Benjamin Jowett

"Trust the man who hesitates in his speech and is quick and steady in action, but beware of long arguments and long beards."

George Santayana

"In the darkest hours we must believe in ourselves."

Terry Goodkind

"To be good and to do good, that is the whole of religion."

Swami Vivekananda

"A little philosophy inclineth man's mind to atheism, but depth in philosophy bringeth men's minds about to religion."

Francis Bacon

"My religion is based on truth and non-violence. Truth is my God. Non-violence is the means of realising Him."

Mahatma Gandhi

"Distinguish between creed and faith."

Swami Ramtirtha

"People are very fond giving away what they need most themselves. It is what I call the depths of generosity."

Oscar Wilde (on Advice)

"Trust takes years to build, seconds to break, and forever to repair."

Yoddler

"Science without religion is lame. Religion without science is blind."

Albert Einstein

"Faith consists in believing when it is beyond the power of reason to believe."

Voltaire

"Let your faith be bigger than your fear."

Heidi Lamberton

"Replace fear with faith, and fear will disappear."

Billy Cox

"Faith, faith, faith in ourselves, faith, faith in God - this is the secret of greatness."

Swami Vivekananda

"I trust God with my life . . . . After all, he gave it to me."

Sherry James

"Faith tells me that no matter what lies ahead of me, God is already there."

Eric Tabs

"Religion is an excellent means of keeping common man quiet".

Napolean Bonaparte

"Faith is the bird that feels the light and sings when the dawn is still dark."

Rabindranath Tagore

"Have faith yourselves, and stand up on that faith and be strong; that is what we need."

Swami Vivekananda

"I like the religion that teaches liberty, equality and fraternity."

B.R. Ambedkar

"God has not called me to be successful. He called me to be faithful."

Mother Teresa

"God has no religion."

Mahatma Gandhi

"Faith is taking the first step even when you can't see the whole staircase."

Martin Luther King

"Religion is a mere ritual for most Indians. People in India, generally practice religion in an external way or for money."

Mary Pat Fisher

"Sovereign cure for worry is religious faith".

William James

"To be trusted is a greater compliment than to be loved."

George MacDonald

"Your daily life is your temple and your religion."

Kahlil Gibran

"In situations where man is helpless, faith in God and His blessings work wonders."

Ashok Sawhney

17

Friends and Foes

"In a battle a soldier went to bring his wounded friend back from field. His captain said,
'It's of no use! Your friend must be dead.'
But soldier still goes and brings back his friend's dead body
Seeing the dead body, the captain says
'I told you, its of no worth. He's dead.'
The soldier replies, 'No sir, it was really worth. When I got to him, my friend saw me, smiled & said his last words – I knew you would surely come.'
The is friendship."

"Friendship after business is better than business after friendship."

Ashok Sawhney

"A single rose can be my garden . . . a single friend, my world."

Leo Buscaglia

"A real friend is one who walks in when the rest of the world walks out."

Walter Winchell

"You have enemies?
Good. That means you have stood up for something, sometime in your life."

Winston Churchill

"Keep acquaintance with all, friendship with some, but intimacy with one."

Swami Vivekananda

"If you go looking for a friend, you're going to find they're very scarce. If you go out to be a friend, you'll find them everywhere."

Zig Ziglar

"You can make more friends in two months by becoming interested in other people, than you can in two years by trying to get other people interested in you."

Dale Carnegie

"True friendship is like sound health, the value of it seldom known until it be lost."

Charles Caleb Colton

"The only way to have a friend is to be one."

Ralph Waldo Emerson

"Friendship increases in visiting friends, but in visiting them seldom."

Thomas Fuller

"Friendship is love without his wings."

Lord Byron

"Friendship may and often does grow into love, but love never subsides into friendship."

Lord Byron

"By force hath overcome but half his foe."

John Milton

"I didn't find my friends; the good God gave them to me."

Ralph Waldo Emerson

"Silences make the real conversations between friends. Not the saying but the never needing to say is what counts."

Margaret Lee Runbeck

"Animals are my friends . . . and I don't eat my friends."

George Bernard Shaw

"People are lonely because they build walls instead of bridges."

Joseph Fort Newton

"In prosperity our friends know us, in adversity we know our friends."

John Churton Collins

"What is the good of friendship if one cannot say exactly what one means."

Oscar Wilde

"Our enemies come nearer the truth in the judgment they form of us, than we do in our judgment of ourselves."

La Rochefoucauld

"Our chief want in life is someone who shall make us do what we can. This is the service of a friend. With him we are easily great."

Ralph Waldo Emerson

"Friendship improves happiness and abates misery, by the doubling of our joys, and the dividing of our grief."

Marchs Tullius Cicero

"Between men and women there is no friendship possible. There is passion, enmity, worship, love, but no friendship."

Oscar Wilde

"The friends thou hast, and their adoption tried, grapple them to thy soul with hoops of steel."

William Shakespeare

"An acquaintance that begins with a compliment is sure to develop into a real friendship. It starts in the right manner."

Oscar Wilde

"Strangers are friends that you have yet to meet."

Roberta Lieberman

"One has a right to judge a man by the effect he has over his friends."

Oscar Wilde

"No friendship is an accident."

O. Henry

"I would rather walk with a friend in the dark, than alone in the light."

Helen Keller

"You can sympathise with the sufferings of a friend, but it requires a very fine nature to sympathise with a friend's success."

Oscar Wilde

"Don't walk behind me; I may not lead. Don't walk in front of me; I may not follow. Just walk beside me and be my friend."

Albert Camus

"The best mirror is an old friend."

George Herbert

"It takes a great deal of courage to stand up to your enemies, but a great deal more to stand up to your friends."

J.K. Rowling

"Wishing to be friends is quick work, but friendship is a slow ripening fruit."

Aristotle

"A friend to all is a friend to none."

Aristotle

"Friendship is delicate as a glass, once broken it can be fixed but there will always be cracks."

Waqar Ahmed

"Be slow to fall into friendship, but when you are in, continue firm and constant."

Socrates

"Some people go to priests. Others to poetry. I to my friends."

Virginia Woolf

"I get by with a little help from my friends."

The Beatles

"An insincere and evil friend is more to be feared than a wild beast; a wild beast may wound your body, but an evil friend will wound your mind."

Buddha

"Friends should be like books, few, but hand-selected."

C. J. Langenhoven

"A friend is someone who can see the truth and pain in you even when you are fooling everyone else."

Scrapbook.com

"Never explain yourself. Your friends don't need it and your enemies won't believe it."

Belgicia Howell

"Friendship isn't about whom you have known the longest . . . . It's about who came, and never left your side."

Mikaela Tiu

"If you live to be 100, I hope I live to be 100 minus 1 day, so I never have to live without you."

Winnie the Pooh

"A true friend never gets in your way unless you happen to be going down."

Arnold H. Glasgow

"I don't need a friend who changes when I change and who nods when I nod; my shadow does that much better."

Plutarch

"Tis the privilege of friendship to talk nonsense, and to have her nonsense respected."

Charles Lamb

"Friendship is the only cement that will ever hold the world together."

Woodrow T. Wilson

"Friends are those rare people who ask how we are and then wait to hear the answer."

Ed Cunningham

"The most beautiful discovery true friends make is that they can grow separately without growing apart."

Elisabeth Foley

"A good friend can tell you what is the matter with you in a minute. He may not seem such a good friend after telling."

Arthur Brisbane

"It is not so much our friends' help that helps us, as the confidence of their help."

Epicurus

"The best time to make friends is before you need them."

Ethel Barrymore

"Truly great friends are hard to find, difficult to leave, and impossible to forget."

Selena Gomez

"One of the most beautiful qualities of true friendship is to understand and to be understood."

Lucius Annaeus Seneca

"Friendship is always a sweet responsibility, never an opportunity."

Khalil Gibran

"It is one of the blessings of old friends that you can afford to be stupid with them."

Ralph Waldo Emerson

"True friendship is when you walk into their house and your WiFi connects automatically."

Alan Garner

"Friendship is like money, easier made than kept."

Samuel Butler

"A friend is someone who knows all about you and still loves you."

Elbert Hubbard

"My best friend is the one who brings out the best in me."

Henry Ford

"Friends are the family you choose."

Jess C. Scott

"A friendship that can end, never really began."

Publilius Syrus

"A friend is one of the nicest things you can have, and one of the best things you can be."

Douglas Pagels

"Friendship is of so sweet and steady and loyal and enduring a nature that it will last through a whole lifetime, if not asked to lend money."

Mark Twain

"The most I can do for my friend is simply, to be his friend."

Henry David Thoreau

"One best book is equal to hundred good friends, one good friend is equal to a library."

A. P. J. Abdul Kalam

"A friend in power is a friend lost."

Henry Brooks

"In the end, we remember the words of our enemies, but the silence of our friends."

Martin Luther King

"Friendship can only be expected between two equals."

Swami Vivekananda

"Give 1000 chances to your enemy to become your friend. But don't give a single chance to your friend to be your enemy."

Hazrat Ali

"God never created friends with price tags."

Rush Tal

"Depth of friendship does not depend on length of acquaintance."

Rabindranath Tagore

"Good Friends should be like
two zeros <0, 0>
when you try to add, they are same and
when you subtract, they are again same
but when you try two divide, they are 'INDIVISIBLE.'"

Anonymous

"The more arguments you win, the less friends you will have."

E.F.L. Wood

"I am wealthy in my friends."

William Shakespeare

"Friendship is born at that moment when one person says to another: 'what! You too? I thought I was the only one.'"

C.S. Lewis

"It's easy to make friends, but hard to get rid to them."

Mark Twain

"Good friends show their love in times of trouble, not just in times of happiness."

Euripides

"There is nothing on this earth more to be prized than true friendship."

Mark Twain

"If you have one true friend, you have more than your share."

Thomas Fuller

"You cannot shake hands with a clenched fist."

Indira Gandhi

"Perfect is the enemy of good."

Voltaire

"Never interrupt your enemy when he is making a mistake."

Napoleon Bonaparte

"A wise man gets more use from his enemies than a fool from his friends."

Baltasar Gracian

"A man cannot be too careful in the choice of his enemies."

Oscar Wilde

"A false friend and a shadow attend only while the sun shines."

Benjamin Franklin

"Let us never try to get even with our enemies because if we do, we will hurt ourselves far more than we hurt them."

Dwight D. Eisenhower

"Friendship is more needed by the happy than the unhappy for happiness is multiplied by being shared."

Aristotle

"Animals are such agreeable friends – they ask no questions, they pass no criticism."

George Eliot

"Only those who care about you can hear you when you're quiet."

Kushand Wizdom

"Why is propaganda so much more successful when it stirs up hatred than when it tries to stir up friendly feeling?"

Bertrand Russell

"Kill the enemity, and not the enemy."

Ashok Sawhney

18

Gifts

"Give what you have. To someone, it may be better than you dare to think."

Henry Wadsworth Longfellow

"I have held many things in my hands, and I have lost them all; but whatever I have placed in God's hands, that I still possess."

Martin Luther King

"God's gifts put man's best dreams to shame."

Elizabeth Barrett Browning

"Ever be grateful to God for having given you the precious gift of 'Life' ."

Ashok Sawhney

"Some of most valuable gifts come wrapped in the ugliest paper."

Navonne Johns

"For it is in giving that we receive."

Francis of Assisi

"You can give without loving, but you cannot love without giving."

Amy Carmichael

"The manner of giving is worth more than the gift."

Pierre Corneille, Le Menteur

"Real pleasure according to me, does not lie in getting, but in giving."

Ashok Sawhney

19

Goodness and Kindness

"They alone live who live for others, the rest are more dead than alive."

Swami Vivekananda

"It's nice to be important but it's more important to be nice."

John Templeton

"The sincere alone can recognise sincerity."

Thomas Carlyle

"Be helpful and kinder to people, they may be fighting harder life's battles than you could imagine."

Ashok Sawhney

"God has put something noble and good into every heart which His hand created."

Mark Twain

"When men give up saying what is charming, they give up thinking what is charming."

Oscar Wilde

"Conviction is worthless unless it is converted into conduct."

Thomas Carlyle

"This is the gist of all worship – to be pure and to do good to others."
Swami Vivekananda

"Be not simply good; be good for something."
Henry David Thoreau

"Good actions are the invisible hinges on the doors of heaven."
Victor Hugo

"Doing good in return for evil is the correct morality."
Socrates

"We like people in proportion to the good we do them and not to the good they do us."
Laurence Sterne

"Have you had a kindness shown? Pass it on."
Henry Burton

"He is gentil that doth gentil deeds."
Will Durant

"The best portion of a goodman's life: his little, nameless, unremembered acts of kindness and of love."
William Wordsworth

"Three things in human life are important: the first is to be kind; the second is to be kind; and the third is to be kind."
Henry James

"The best way to find yourself is to lose yourself in the service of others."
Mahatma Gandhi

"Good actions give strength to ourselves and inspire good actions in others."

Plato

"He who is too busy doing good, finds no time to be good."

Rabindranath Tagore

"The greatest good you can do for another is not just to share your riches but to reveal to him his own."

Benjamin Disraeli

"True charity is the desire to be useful to others without thought of recompense."

Emanuel Swedenborg

"Write the injuries done to you by others on sand, but engrave the least goodness done to you by others on marble."

Swami Vivekananda

"Be nice to people on your way up, because you meet the same people on your way down."

Jimmy Durante

"He who wants to do good knocks at the gate; he who loves finds the gate open."

Rabindranath Tagore

"We ourselves feel that what we are doing is just a drop in the ocean. But the ocean would be less because of that missing drop."

Mother Teresa

"It is a long Journey, between human being and being human. Think twice."

Osho

"There is no limit to the amount of good you can do if you don't care who gets the credit."

Ronald Reagan

"Every man is guilty of all the good he did not do."

Voltaire

"How good life is when one does something good and just!"

Fyodor Dostoyevsky

"Kind words can be short and easy to speak, but their echoes are truly endless."

Mother Teresa

"There is no exercise better for the heart than reaching down and lifting people up."

John Holmes

"The earth is nobler than the world we have put upon it."

J.B. Priestly

"Those who bring sunshine to the lives of others, cannot keep it from themselves."

J.M. Barrie

"Being nice is one of many bridges on the road to happiness."

Donna A. Favors

"A good deed done with a wrong motive may benefit others, but will in the end be harmful to the doer's mind."

Lord Budha

"Coffee never knew it will taste nice and sweet, before it met sugar and milk. We are good as individuals but become better when we blend with the right people. The world is full of nice people. If you can't find one, be one."

Loyan

"Be good to people for no reason."

Tiny Buddha

"There is nothing stronger in the world than gentleness."

Han Suyin

"There is no charm equal to tenderness of heart."

Jane Austen

"If you want to know what a man's like, take a good look at how he treats his inferiors, not his equals."

J.K. Rowling

"Spread love everywhere you go. Let no one ever come to you without leaving happier."

Mother Teresa

"I have learned silence from the talkative, toleration from the intolerant, and kindness from the unkind."

Khalil Gibran

"How you make others feel about themselves, says a lot about you."

Berta Lippert

"Nobody has ever become poor by doing acts of charity."

Ashok Sawhney

20

Happiness, Sadness, Laughter, Smile and Tears

"A man asked Gautam Buddha,
'I want happiness.'
Buddha said, 'first remove 'I' that's ego, then remove 'want' that's desire. See now you are left with
only Happiness."

Gautam Buddha

"What sunshine is to flowers, smiles are to humanity."

Joseph Addison

"What's the use of worrying
it never was worthwhile, so,
pack up your troubles in your old kit-bag,
and smile, smile, smile."

George Henry Powell

"One may smile, and smile and be a villain."

William Shakespeare

"He who avoids extremes, in feed and fast, in sleep and waking, and in work and play, he winneth yoga, balance, peace and joy."

Bhagavad Gita

"Every one can master grief but he that has it."

William Shakespeare

"Grief is a species of idleness."

Samuel Johnson

"Pleasure is oft a visitant; but pain, clings cruelly to us."

John Keats

"'Tis held that sorrow makes us wise."

Alfred Lord Tennyson

"It is not easy to find happiness in ourselves, and it is not possible to find it elsewhere."

Agnes Repplier

"Since you get more joy out of giving joy to others, you should put a good deal of thought into the happiness that you are able to give."

Eleanor Roosevelt

"One of the sanest, surest, and most generous joys of life comes from being happy over the good fortune of others."

Archibald Rutledge

"The only way on earth to multiply happiness is to divide it."

Paul Schererst

"That state of life is most happy where superfluities are not required and necessities are not wanting."

Plutarch

"Variety is the mother of enjoyment."

Benjamin Disraeli

"Grief makes one hour ten."

William Shakespeare

"Happiness is the full use of your powers, along lines of excellence in life affording scope."

John F. Kennedy

"I don't trust anyone who doesn't laugh."

Maya Angelou

"Happiness never decreases by being shared."

Gautam Budha

"In tragedy every moment is eternity; in comedy eternity is a moment."

Christopher Fry

"There is nothing in the world so irresistibly contagious as laughter and good humor."

Charles Dickens

"If thou wilt make a man happy, add not unto his riches, but take away from his desires."

Epicurus

"Sweet is pleasure after pain."

John Dryden

"Though sages may pour out their wisdom's treasure; there is no sterner moralist than pleasure."

Lord Byron

"Remember happiness doesn't depend upon who you are or what you have. It depends solely upon what you think."

Dale Carnegie

"Learn to laugh at your troubles and you'll never run out of things to laugh at."

Lyn Karol

"If you see someone without a smile, give them one of yours."

Dolly Parton

"Happiness and beauty are by-products."

George Bernard Shaw

"Laughter is an instant vacation."

Milton Berle

"Realise that happiness can never be found in the mere rearrangement of exterior conditions."

Vernon Howard

"There is only one way to happiness and that is to cease worrying about things which are beyond the power of our will."

Epictetus

"Sometimes your joy is the source of your smile, but sometimes your smile can be the source of your joy."

Thich Nhat Hanh

"Happiness is when what you think, what you say, and what you do are in harmony."

Mahatma Gandhi

"Some cause happiness wherever they go; others whenever they go."

Oscar Wilde

"Happiness is not something ready-made. It comes from your own actions."

Dalai Lama

"When one door of happiness closes, another opens, but often we look so long at the closed door that we do not see the one that has been opened for us."

Helen Keller

"The secret of being miserable is to have leisure to bother about whether you are happy or not. The cure for it is occupation."

George Bernard Shaw

"Happiness depends upon ourselves."

Aristotle

"The secret of happiness is not in doing what one likes, but in liking what one does."

James M. Barrie

"When we are happy we are always good but when we are good we are not always happy."

Oscar Wilde

"The unhappy derive comfort from the misfortunes of others."

Aesop

"Happy he who learns to bear what he cannot change."

Friedrich Schiller

"I'd far rather be happy than right any day."

Douglas Adams

"The foolish man seeks happiness in the distance, the wise grows it under his feet."

James Oppenheim

"Action may not always bring happiness; but there is no happiness without action."

Benjamin Disraeli

"Happiness is nothing more than a good health and a bad memory."

Albert Schweitzer

"Our envy always lasts longer than the happiness of those we envy."

Heraclitus

"Happiness always looks small while you hold it in your hands, but let it go, and you learn at once how big and precious it is."

Maxim Gorky

"Do not spoil what you have by desiring what you have not; remember that what you now have was once among the things you only hoped for."

Epicurus

"A lifetime of happiness? No man alive could bear it; it would be hell on earth."

George Bernard Shaw

"The most wasted of all days is one without laughter."

E.E. Cummings

"Laughter is the shortest distance between two people."

Victor Borge

"The happiest of people don't necessarily have the best of everything; They just make the best of everything they have."

Tiny Budda

"Happiness is time spent with good friends."

Mark Twain

"Most people are about as happy as they make up their minds to be."

Abraham Lincoln

"A man is happy so long as he chooses to be happy."

Alexander Solzhenitsyn

"Happiness is inward not outward. It does not depend on what we have, but on what we are."

Henry Van Dyke

"Laugh to forget but don't forget to laugh."

Arnold Glasow

"Being happy does not mean everything's perfect, it means you've decided to look beyond the imperfections."

Gerard Way

"Those who complain little are happiest in life."

Ashok Sawhney

"Everyone wants happiness; no one needs pain! But it is not possible to get a rainbow without a little rain."

Zion Lee

"The smile that flickers on baby's lips when he sleeps."

Rabindranath Tagore

"Grief can take care of itself, but to get the full value of joy you must have somebody to divide it with."

Mark Twain

"Plant a seed of friendship; reap a bouquet of happiness."

Lois L. Kaufman

"A single finger which wipes your tears during your grief, is much better than the ten fingers which come together to clap on your success."

Irfaan Nazir Akash

"Always be the reason of someone's happiness, never just a part of it, be a part of someone's sadness, but never be the reason for it."

Aldyna Threesya

"Define the word 'birthday'? Answer: The only day in your life, when you cried and your mother was smiling."

Dr. A.P.J. Abdul Kalam

"'The sweetest couple in the world is
'Smile and Tears.'
They rarely meet but when they do
the moment becomes unforgettable."

Elie Ferzil

"Smile and the world smiles with you; cry, and you cry alone."

Jack Ellison

"Happiness is the best makeup."

Drew Barrymore

"Happiness is not something readymade. It comes from your own actions."

Dalai Lama

"Tears can be more special than smiles, for smiles can be given to anyone but tears are shed for people we love."

Anonymous

"Why are you sad?"
"Because you speak to me in words and I look at you with feelings."

Leo Tolstoy

"Those who weep recover more quickly than those who smile."

Jean Girandoux

"Growth itself contains the germs of happiness."

Pearl S. Buck

"A good deed is one which brings a smile of joy to the face of another."

Prophet Mohd.

"A smile is a curve which can set a lot of things straight."

Phyllis Diller

"When you're happy you enjoy the music. When you're sad you understand the lyrics."

Frank Ocean

"With the fearful strain that is on me night and day, if I did not laugh I should die."

Abraham Lincoln

"Laughter is a tranquilizer with no side effects."

Arnold Glasow

"Ensure that you give maximum happiness to people you love, even if they hurt you."

Ashok Sawhney

21

Helpfulness and Selfishness

"It is better to light a candle than to curse the darkness."

Eleanor Roosevelt

"The greatest object in the universe, says a certain philosopher, is a good man struggling with adversity; yet there is a still greater, which is the good man that comes to relieve it."

Oliver Goldsmith

"A forced favour deserves no gratitude."

Ashok Sawhney

"I sought to hear the voice of God and climbed the topmost steeple, but God declared: 'Go down again – I dwell among the people.'"

John Henry Newman

"When bad men combine, the good must associate, else they will fall one by one."

Edmund Burke

"The hardest reality of life is that, when you need advice, everyone is ready to help you, but when you need help, everyone is ready to advice you."

Marc and Angel

"Extending one hand to help somebody has more value; than joining two hands for prayer. . . ."

Sunny Rai

"A little bit of fragrance always clings to the hand that gives you roses."

Robin Sharma

"What we have done for ourselves alone dies with us: what we have done for others and the world, remains and is immortal."

Albert Pike

"To live a pure unselfish life, one must count nothing as one's own in the midst of abundance."

Buddha

"Help yourself by helping others."

John Templeton

"Condemn none: if you can stretch out a helping hand, do so. If you cannot, fold your hands, bless your brothers, and let them go their own way."

Swami Vivekananda

"A banker is a fellow who lends you his umbrella when the sun is shining but wants it back the minute it begins to rain."

Mark Twain

"There are two ways of spreading light: to be the candle or the mirror that reflects it."

Edith Wharton

"Try not to become a man of success, but rather try to become a man of value."

Albert Einstein

"Try to be a rainbow in someone's cloud."

Maya Angelou

"No one is useless in this world who lightens the burdens of another."

Charles Dickens

"I come in a world of iron . . . to make a world of gold."

Dale Wasserman

"One of the most important things you can do on this earth is to let people know they are not alone."

Shannon L. Alder

"Forget yourself by becoming interested in other's welfare."

Dale Carnegie

"Spiritual life is complete selflessness."

Shivanand

"Never refuse to help someone. You might be the only one that does."

Ashok Sawhney

22

Home and House

"Let parents bequeath will to their children not riches, but the spirit of reverence."

Plato

"Anyone can build an altar; it requires a God to provide the flame. Anybody can build a house; we need the Lord for the creation of a home."

John Henry Jowett

"The Christian home is the Master's workshop where the processes of character molding are silently, lovingly, faithfully, and successfully carried on."

Lord Houghton

"Home life is no more natural to us than a cage is natural to a cockatoo."

George Bernard Shaw

"I dislike feeling at home when I am abroad."

George Bernard Shaw

"A house is not a home."

Polly Adler

"These are days of fancier houses but broken homes."

Bob Moorehead

"A good neighbour doubles the value of a house."

G.K. Chesterten

"No government program, no social service, no speech by a public official is substitute for interest at home, inspiration at home, encouragement at home."

H.B. Humphrey

"A home is like a school where we learn from each other. It is an extension of our bodies in a way."

Ashok Sawhney

23

Hope, Worry and Despair

"When you go to bed at night, have for your pillow three things– love, hope and forgiveness. And you will awaken in the morning with a song in your heart."

Victor Hugo

"If you have built castles in the air, your work need not be lost;
that is where they should be, now put foundations under them."

Henry David Thoreau

"Whoever falls from God's right hand is caught into his left."

Edwin Markham

"Our humanity were a poor thing were it not for the divinity that stirs within us."

Francis Bacon

"Nothing is more dangerous than an idea, when it is the only one we have."

Alain Chartier

"If seeds in the black earth can turn into such beautiful roses, what might not the heart of man become in its long journey toward the stars?"

Gilbert Keith Chesterton

"To mourn a mischief that is past and gone, is the next way to draw mischief on."

William Shakespeare

"We must accept finite disappointment, but we must never lose infinite hope."

Martin Luther King Jr.

"A 'hope' and an 'end', they are always there. It depends on us how we deal with them. We can look at it as a hopeless end or an endless hope."

Vibhu Batra

"I am an optimist. It does not seem too much use being anything else."

Winston Churchill

"Worry never robs tomorrow of its sorrow, it only saps today of its joy."

Leo Buscaglia

"Worry is like a rocking chair, it gives you something to do but never gets you anywhere."

Erma Bombeck

"Karl Marx was the man who himself lived in misery, gave the world the hope for the complete abolition of poverty."

Robert B. Down

"One small positive thought in the morning can change your whole day."

Zig Ziglar

"A single thread of hope is still a very powerful thing."

John Brown

"There is no place like hope."

Vickie Girard

"Hope is the only thing stronger than fear."

Suzanne Collins

"Frustration is the child of expectation. Whenever you expect, frustration is bound to come."

Ashok Sawhney

24

Morality, Immortality, Joy and Humanity

"I believe in the immortality of the soul because I have within me immortal longings."

Helen Keller

"Heaven often seems distant and unknown, but if He who made the road thither is our guide, we need not fear to lose the way."

Henry Van Dyke

"They who never melt with pity, never melt with love."

Thomas Moore

"Real joy comes not from ease or riches or from the praise of men, but from doing something worthwhile."

Wilfred T. Grenfell

"The nice thing about meditation is that it makes doing nothing quite respectable."

Paul Dean

"Immoral women are rarely attractive. What made her quite irresistible was that she was unmoral."

Oscar Wilde

"Let us be of good cheer, remembering that the misfortunes hardest to bear are those which never come."

Amy Lowell

"You must not lose faith in humanity. Humanity is like an ocean; if a few drops of the ocean are dirty, the ocean does not become dirty."

Mahatma Gandhi

"If the cask is to hold wine, its water must first be poured out."

Ellen F. Davis

"You truly love, when you feel one with all."

Gautam Buddha

"Doing good in return for evil is the correct morality."

Socrates

"What is morally wrong cannot be politically right."

William Ewart Gladstone

"The guilty think all talk is of themselves."

Geoffrey Chaucer

"Those who feel guilty are afraid, and they who are afraid somehow feel guilty."

Eric Hoffer

"Spirituality alone is real power."

Shivanand

"What lies behind us and what lies before us are tiny matters compared to what lies within us."

Henry Stanley Haskins

"Ideals never die."

Sister Nivedita

"He reminds me of the person who murdered his parents, and when sentence was about to be pronounced, pleaded for mercy on the ground that he was an orphan."

Abraham Lincoln

"The beauty on the inside, will determine the ugly on the outside."

Anthony Liccione

"Be grateful to Him for every sacred breath. The next may not come."

Ashok Sawhney

25

Life and Death

"The only thing you take with you when you're gone is what you leave behind."

John Aliston

"A long life may not be good enough but a good life is long enough."

Benjamin Franklin

"Life is a pure flame, and we live by an invisible sun within us."

Thomas Browne

"Life is a series of surprises, and would not be worth taking or keeping, if it were not."

Ralph Waldo Emerson

"The great use of life is to spend it for something that outlasts it."

William James

"A life spent making mistakes is not only more honorable, but more useful than a life spent doing nothing."

George Bernard Shaw

"Death is but a pause in the cycle of life."

Ashok Sawhney

"Be a life long or short, its completeness depends on what it was lived for."

David Starr Jordan

"Alcohol is the anesthesia by which we endure the operation of life."

George Bernard Shaw

"Everyone is trying to accomplish something big, not realising that life is made up of little things."

Frank A. Clark

"The only way a woman can ever reform a man is by boring him so completely that he loses all possible interest in life."

Oscar Wilde

"We love life, not because we are used to living, but because we are used to loving."

Friedrich Nietzsche

"The best thing to hold onto life is each other."

Audrey Hepburn

"All our lives we sweat and save, building for a shallow grave."

Jim Morrison

"In school you are taught a lesson and then give a test, in life - you're given a test that teaches you a lesson."

Tom Bodett

"Ups and downs in life are very important to keep us going, because a straight line even in an E.C.G. means we are not alive."

Ratan Tata

"This life is a keepsake of death."

Ashok Sawhney

"He that dies pays all debts."

William Shakespeare

"One of the fathers saith that old men go to death and death comes to young men."

Francis Bacon

"Cowards die many times before their death, the valiant never taste death but once."

William Shakespeare

"Death, in itself, is nothing; but we fear. To be we know not what, we know not where."

John Dryden

"The best of men cannot suspend their fate; the good die early, and the bad die late."

Daniel Defoe

"Truth sits upon the lips of dying men."

Matthew Arnold

"I am about to take my last voyage, a great leap in the dark."

Thomas Hobbes

"So little done, so much to do."

Cecil Rhodes

"The world's an inn, and death the journey's end."

John Dryden

"There is no death. What appears so, is only re-incarnation."

Ashok Sawhney

"Let us endeavor so to live that when we come to die even the undertaker will be sorry."

Mark Twain

"Don't try to live forever. You will not succeed."

George Bernard Shaw

"The one who plants trees, knowing that he will never sit in their shade, has at least started to understand the meaning of life."

Rabindranath Tagore

"I have a strong feeling that I shall be glad when I am dead and done for - scrapped at last to make room for somebody better, cleverer, more perfect than myself."

George Bernard Shaw

"One crowded hour of glorious life is worth an age without a name."

T.O. Mordaunt

"I live with gusto and enthusiasm. I live every day as if it were, the first day I had ever seen and the last day I was going to see."

Dr. Lynn Phelps

"If you cry because the sun has gone out of your life, your tears will prevent you from seeing the stars."

Rabindranath Tagore

"I want to be thoroughly used up when I die, for the harder I work the more I live. I rejoice in life for its own sake."

George Bernard Shaw

"It is our virtuous qualities and not where we are born, that makes us great."

Ashok Sawhney

"There is no cure for birth and death, save to enjoy the interval."

George Santayana

"Life is really simple, but we insist on making it complicated."

Confucius

"Life levels all men. Death reveals the eminent."

George Bernard Shaw

"There is more to life than increasing its speed."

Mahatma Gandhi

"Life is given to us, we earn it by giving it."

Rabindranath Tagore

"Life is partly what we make it, and partly what it is made by the friends we choose."

Tennessee Williams

"You only live once, but if you do it right, once is enough."

Mae West

"In three words I can sum up everything I've learned about life: it goes on."

Robert Frost

"Life isn't about finding yourself. Life is about creating yourself."

Albert Einstein

"Life is like riding a bicycle. To keep your balance, you must keep moving."

Albert Einstein

"When I hear somebody sigh, 'Life is hard,' I am always tempted to ask, 'Compared to what?'"

Sydney Harris

"Life has two rules:
#1 Never quit
#2 Always remember rule # 1."

Duke Ellington

"It's a funny thing about life; if you refuse to accept anything but the best, you very often get it."

Somerset Maugham

"Death does not concern us, because as long as we exist, death is not here. And when it does come, we no longer exist."

Epicurus

"When you get little, you want more. When you get more, you desire even more. But when you lose it, you realize little was enough."

T.S. Eliot

"God made woman beautiful and foolish. Beautiful that man might love her and foolish that she might love him."

William Shakespeare

"This life is not for complaint but for satisfaction."

Henry David Thoreau

"What is the meaning of life? To be happy and useful."

Dalai Lama

"We live if we love our life."

Rabindranath Tagore

"Death is not the greatest loss in life. The greatest loss is what dies inside us while we live."

Norman Cousins

"Most people would rather die than think, and they do."

George Bernard Shaw

"The fear of death follows from the fear of life. A man who lives fully is prepared to die at any time."

Mark Twain

"We all die. The goal isn't to live forever, the goal is to create something that will."

Chuck Palahniuk

"Sometimes in life we think we don't need anyone, but when we need someone we don't have anyone. So don't let your best friends go."

Anonymous

"When someone says
'You've changed.'
It simply means
you've stopped
living your life
their way."

Bianca Barton

"The two most important days in your life are the day you are born and the day you find out why."

Mark Twain

"Life is a succession of lessons which must be lived to be understood."

Helen Keller

"I asked Life: Why are you so difficult?
Life smiled and said, 'You people never appreciate easy things.'"

Buddha

"Life is not measured by the number of breaths we take, but by the moments that take our breath away."

Maya Angelou

"Generosity is not in giving me that which I need more than you do, but it is in giving me that which you need more than I do."

Kahlil Gibran

"A single death is a tragedy, a million deaths is a statistic."

Joseph Stalin

"Grief does not change you . . . It reveals you."

John Green

"As a well spent day brings happy sleep, so life well used brings happy death."

Leonardo da Vinci

"Life is not fair, get used to it."

Bill Gates

"We have learned how to make a living but not a life. We have added years to life, not life to years."

Bob Moorehead

"We are always getting ready to live, but never living."

Ralph Waldo Emerson

"I am certain that I have been here as I am now, a thousand times before and I hope to return."

Goethe

"An ordinary life is the base for spiritual advancement."

Lord Mahavira

"Retain your calmness. Ordinary life is like a pendulum, ceaselessly swinging back and forth."

Swami Yoganand

"He lives in fame that dies in virtue's cause."

William Shakespeare

"To live in hearts we leave behind is not to die."

Thomas Campbell

"No man's story of his own life can fail to be of interest to other, if it is written in sincerity."

Dr. Radhakrishnan

"Life is a pilgrimage to God."

Satya Sai Baba

"The web of our life is of a mingled yarn, good and ill together."

William Shakespeare

"For not to live at ease is not to live."

John Dryden

"Every moment dies a man, every moment one is born."

Alfred Lord Tennyson

"Death is the fairest thing in the world. No one's ever gotten out of it. The earth takes everyone - the kind, the cruel, the sinners. Aside from that, there's no fairness on earth."

Svetlana Alexievich

"Self-reverence, self-knowledge, self-control, these three alone lead life to sovereign power."

Alfred Lord Tennyson

"Brief is life but love is long."

Alfred Lord Tennyson

"To expect life to treat you good is as foolish as hoping a bull won't hit you because you are a vegetarian."

Roseanne Barr

"When one has a grateful heart, life becomes easy and graceful."

Ashok Sawhney

26

Love, Hate and Affection

"A dog is the only thing on earth that loves you more than you love yourself."

Josh Billings

"Love is a tonic."

Albert Hubert

"Love's the noblest frailty of the mind."

John Dryden

"Love's a malady without a cure."

John Dryden

"The love of liberty is the love of others; the love of power is the love of ourselves."

William Hazlitt

"Absense sharpens love, presence strengthens it."

Thomas Fuller

"Who ever loved, that loved not at first sight?"

Christopher Marlowe

"People will hurt you, only if you allow them to. Don't settle for less when you know you deserve the best."

Rashida Rowe

"When you care for someone more than they deserve, you get hurt more than you deserve."

Nishan Panwar

"Love gives itself; it is not bought."

Henry Wadsworth Longfellow

"A wise love values not so much the gift of the lover as the love of the giver."

Thomas K. Kempis

"Love cures people – both the ones who give it and the ones who receive it."

Karl A. Menninger

"All mankind love a lover."

Ralph Waldo Emerson

"A loving heart is the beginning of all knowledge."

Thomas Carlyle

"Love does not consist in gazing at each other, but in looking outward together in the same direction."

Antoine De Saint-Exupery

"Love is an endless mystery, for it has nothing else to explain it."

Rabindranath Tagore

"Two persons who love each other are in a place more holy than the interior of a church."

William Lyon Phelps

"Love is not blind – it sees more, not less, but because it sees more, it is willing to see less."

Julius Cordon

"He loves each one of us, as if there were only one of us."

St. Augustine

"I hate people who talk about themselves, as you do, when one wants to talk about oneself, as I do."

Oscar Wilde

"I like not only to be loved, but to be told that I am loved; the realm of silence is large enough beyond the grave."

George Eliot

"There is no sincerer love than the love of food."

George Bernard Shaw

"Of all the music that reached farthest into heaven, it is the beating of a loving heart."

Henry Ward Beecher

"It is difficult not to be unjust to what one loves."

Oscar Wilde

"You are loved when you are born.
You will be loved when you die.
In between you have to manage!"

Anonymous

"The one who loves you will never leave you, because even if there are hundred reasons to give up, he will find one reason to hold on."

Ratan Tata

"The way to change other's mind is with affection, and not anger."

Dalai Lama

"Hating somebody all day is more tiring than laboring in the fields from sunrise to sunset."

Dr. F.N. Allen

"Love is that condition in which the happiness of another person is essential to your own."

Robert A. Heinlein

"If you would be loved, love, and be loveable."

Benjamin Franklin

"The way to love anything is to realize that it may be lost."

Gilbert K. Chesterton

"It is not a lack of love, but a lack of friendship that makes unhappy marriages."

Friedrich Nietzsche

"You can't blame gravity for falling in love."

Albert Einstein

"A difference of taste in jokes, is a great strain on the affections."

George Eliot

"Love all, but trust a few."

William Shakespeare

"Love is composed of a single soul inhabiting two bodies."

Aristotle

"Darkness cannot drive out darkness; only light can do that. Hate cannot drive out hate; only love can do that."

Martin Luther King

"All, everything that I understand, I understand only because I love."

Leo Tolstoy

"Where there is love there is life."

Mahatma Gandhi

"If we lose love and self respect for each other, this is how we finally die."

Maya Angelou

"Love begins by taking care of the closest ones - the ones at home."

Mother Teresa

"Love is a game that two can play and both win."

Eva Gabor

"Where there is great love, there are always miracles."

Willa Cather

"To love and be loved is the greatest happiness of existence."

Sydney Frankl

"One word frees us of all the weight and pain of life; that word is love."

Sophocles

"Like me or hate me, both are in my favor. If you like me I am in your heart, if you hate me I am in your mind."

Swami Vivekananda

"A poet is a person who is passionately in love with language."

W. H. Auden

"You know it's love when all you want is that person to be happy, even if you're not part of their happiness."

Jean Zheng

"Love does not claim possession, but gives freedom."

Rabindranath Tagore

"The course of true love never did run smooth."

William Shakespeare

"I never knew how to worship, until I knew how to love."

Henry Ward Beecher

"I love myself despite my infinite faults, how can I hate anyone at the glimpse of a few faults."

Swami Vivekananda

"When you fish for love, bait with your heart, not your brain."

Mark Twain

"Love measures our stature: the more we love, the bigger we are."

William Sloane Coffin Jr.

"He who loves fifty people has fifty woes; he who loves no one has no woes."

Buddha

"Love is a yearning of the one for the one."

Sri Aurobindo Ghosh

"Love is when two people know everything about each other and are still friends."

Mark Twain

"There is no true love without jealousy."

Valentino Igat

"Love isn't something you find, it is something that finds you."

Loretta Young

"In the end, it's not the years in your life that count. It's the life in your years."

Abraham Lincoln

"I have found the paradox that if I love until it hurts, then there is no hurt, but only more love."

Mother Teresa

"You yourself, as much as anyone in the entire universe deserve your love and affection."

Buddha

"There can be no deep disappointment where there is not deep love."

Martin Luther King Jr.

"The bank of love is never bankrupt."

Steve Maraboli

"A dog makes his living by giving you nothing but love."

Dale Carnegie

"Confound not love with attachment."

Swamy Ram Tirathi

"Love all, trust a few. Do wrong to none."

William Shakespeare

"If you judge people, you have no time to love them."

Mother Teresa

"Life without love is like a tree without blossoms or fruit."

Khalil Gibran

27

Nation, India, Ballot and Language

"We must have many Lincoln-hearted men."

Vachel Lindsay

"Patriotism is the virtue of the vicious."

Oscar Wilde

"A nation's culture resides in the hearts and in the soul of its people."

Mahatma Gandhi

"A nation that cannot trust its intellectuals cannot trust itself."

Alfred Whitney Griswold

"How grand is India, possessing within her boundaries every kind of beauty! She could not but be the home of a vast and complex civilization."

Sister Nivedita

"The Indian intellect has valued not only belief but doubt."

Indira Gandhi

"Posterity is 'ourselves' according to Hinduism."

Chakrvarti Rajgopalacharya

"I love India as the birthplace of the highest and best of all religions."
Sister Nivedita

"Governments keep their promises only when they are forced or when it is to their advantage to do so."
Napoleon Bonaparte

"A nation is not conquered which is perpetually to be conquered."
Edmund Burke

"Better one suffer, than a nation grieve."
John Dryden

"The reconstitution of a nation has to begin with its ideals."
Sister Nivedita

"The strength of nation is derived from the integrity of its homes."
Confucius

"Those who stay away from the election think that one vote will do no good, it is but one step more to think one vote will do no harm."
Ralph Waldo Emerson

"Ballots are the rightful and peaceful successors to bullets."
Abraham Lincoln

"Our true nationality is mankind."
H.G. Wells

"A nation's greatness is measured by how it treats its weakest members."
Mahatma Gandhi

"Discontent is the first step in the progress of a man or a nation."
Oscar Wilde

"The guilt of a government is the crime of a whole country."

Thomas Paine

"The firm basis of government is justice, not pity."

Woodrow Wilson

"Social prosperity means man happy, the citizen free, the nation great."

Victor Hugo

"The English in India were very honest in things, which were for their benefit."

Pandit Jawaharlal Nehru

"Patriotism is your conviction that this country is superior to all others because you were born in it."

George Bernard Shaw

"Ask not what your country can do for you; ask what you can do for your country."

John F. Kennedy

28

Nature and Science

"Nature is man's religious book, with lessons for every day."

Theodore Parker

"The volume of nature is the book of knowledge."

Oliver Goldsmith

"When nature has work to be done, she creates a genius to do it."

Ralph Waldo Emerson

"I love to think of nature as an unlimited broadcasting station, through which God speaks to us every hour, if we will only tune in."

George Washington Carver

"Nature is the living, visible garment of God."

Johann Wolfgang Von Goethe

"Forests are the lungs of our land, purifying the air and giving fresh strength to people."

Franklin D. Roosevelt

"Dreams come true. Without that possibility, nature would not incite us to have them."

John Updike

"One of the first conditions of happiness is that the link between man and nature shall not be broken."

Leo Tolstoy

"The miracle of a sunrise is that, despite being a predictable event, no two sunrises are ever the same. It's faith renewed; a hope reborn!"

Bukola Babatunde

"A kiss is a lovely trick designed by nature , to stop speech when words become superfluous."

Ingrid Bergman

"Nature gives you the face you have at 20; it is up to you to merit the face you have at 50."

Coco Chanel

"A friend may well be reckoned the masterpiece of nature."

Ralph Waldo Emerson

"To be happy, we must be true to nature, and carry our age along with us."

William Hazlitt

"Science is always wrong. It never solves a problem without creating ten more."

George Bernard Shaw

"Being alone means togetherness, the re-coming together of myself and nature."

Hugh Prather

"Nature never makes anything that is superfluous."

Aristotle

"We still do not know one thousandth of one percent of what nature has revealed to us."

Albert Einstein

"Hidden nature is secret God."

Aurobindo Ghosh

"Nobody can disturb your peace of mind without your permission."

Ashok Sawhney

29

Opportunity, Goal, Variety and Unity

"The pessimist sees the difficulty in every opportunity; the optimist, the opportunity in every difficulty."

Winston Churchill

"We should all be concerned about the future because we will have to spend the rest of our lives there."

Charles F. Kettering

"We are strong in our unity. But we are stronger still because of our diversity."

Richard Nixon

"Three things return not, even for prayers and tears-
The arrow which the archer shoots at will;
The spoken word, keen-edged and sharp to sting;
The opportunity left unimproved.

Opportunity is a bird that never perches."

Claude McDonald

"Opportunity never knocks on the door. You have to knock on opportunity's door, and they are all around you."

Thomas J. Watson

"When you have to make a choice and don't make it, that in itself is a choice."

William James

"Do the hard jobs first. The easy jobs will take care of themselves."

Dale Carnegie

"Things may come to those who wait, but only the things left by those who hustle."

Abraham Lincoln

"The real opportunity for success lies within the person and not in the job."

Zig Ziglar

"A goal is a dream with a deadline."

Napoleon Hill

"If opportunity doesn't knock, build a door."

Miltom Berle

"Arise! Awake! And stop not until the goal is reached."

Swami Vivekananda

"If it doesn't open . . . it's not your door."

Candace Plattor

"Things do not change; we change."

Henry David Thoreau

"Don't wish it were easier, wish you were better."

Jim Rohn

"Be fearful when others are greedy and greedy when others are fearful."

Warren Buffett

"Purpose is the engine that powers and drives life."

B.K. Trehan

"Better to have a bad purpose than no purpose at all."

Thomas Carlyle

"Your dreams must have deadlines to enable you to reach your goals."

Ashok Sawhney

30

War and Peace

"There never was a good war or a bad peace."

Benjamin Franklin

"All delays are dangerous in war."

John Dryden

"Those who are free of resentful thoughts surely find peace."

Buddha

"War is barbarism, militarism is applied barbarism."

Lala Lajpat Rai

"War is the child of pride, and pride the daughter of riches."

Jonathan Swift

"Accurst be he that first invented war."

Christopher Marlowe

"We shall fight on the beaches, we shall fight on the landing grounds, we shall fight in the fields and in the street, we shall fight in the hills, we shall never surrender."

Winston Churchill

"In a true dialogue, both sides are willing to change."

Thick Nhat Hanh

"War is like love, it always finds a way."

Bertolt Brecht

"It takes twenty years or more of the peace to make a man; it takes only twenty seconds war to destroy him."

King Baudouin

"The war to end war was concluded by a peace most beautifully calculated to end peace."

Aldous Leonard Huxley

"The motto of war is: 'Let the strong survive, let the weak die,'
The motto of peace is: 'Let the strong help the weak to survive.'"

Franklin D. Roosevelt

"In war do not hit at all, if it can be avoided, but never hit softly."

Eleanor Roosevelt

"You have to take chances for peace, just as you have to take chances in war."

J. Frank Dobie

"In a battle all you need to make you fight is a little hot blood and the knowledge that it's more dangerous to lose than to win."

George Bernard Shaw

"Peace at any price is not always good. Life is the real thing, not peace and quiet."

Lala Lajpat Rai

"In moderating, not in satisfying desires, lies peace."

Ben Hecht

"If peace cannot be maintained with honour, it is no longer peace."

John Russell

"When peace has been broken anywhere, the peace of all countries everywhere is in danger."

Franklin D. Roosevelt

"Peace cannot be kept by force. It can only be achieved by understanding."

Albert Einstein

"Peace comes from within. Do not seek it without."

Buddha

"When the power of love overcomes the love of power, the world will know peace."

Jimi Hendrix

"First keep the peace within yourself, then you can also bring peace to others."

Thomas A. Kempis

"If you want permanent peace in life, win your enemies with love."

Ashok Sawhney

"In War: Resolution.
In Defeat: Defiance.
In Victory: Magnanimity.
In Peace: Good will."

Winston Churchill

"We do not need guns and bombs to bring peace, we need love and compassion."

Mother Teresa

"Those who are at war with others are not at peace with themselves."

William Hazlitt

"The supreme art of war is to subdue the enemy without fighting."

Sun Tzu

"The purpose of all wars is peace."

Saint Augustine

"Peace and justice are two sides of the same coin."

Dwight D. Eisenhower

"If we have no peace, it is because we have forgotten that we belong to each other."

Mother Teresa

"True peace is not merely the absence of war, it is the presence of justice."

Jane Addams

"It is not possible to achieve peace by force; it can only be attained with love and understanding."

Ashok Sawhney

31

World, Universe, Planet and Earth

"What we have done for ourselves alone dies with us. What we have done for others and the world remains and is immortal."

Albert Pike

"Heaven's joys might have been earth's if earth were pure."

Shri Arvind

"The world hates change, yet it is the only thing that has brought progress."

Charles Kettering

"Our business is to realize the world as we see it, not to reform it as we know it."

Oscar Wilde

"We live in the world when we love it."

Rabindranath Tagore

"All the world's a stage, and all the men and women, merely players."

William Shakespeare

"One half of the world can not understand the pleasures of the other."

Jane Austen

"There is not a joy this world can give like that it takes away."

Lord Byron

"The world is a comedy to those that think, a tragedy to those that feel."

Horace Walpole

"When a man is under the control of senses, he is of the world. When he has controlled the senses, the world is of him."

Swami Vivekananda

"To live is the rarest thing in the world. Most people exist, that is all."

Oscar Wilde

"Old men are dangerous: it doesn't matter to them what is going to happen to the world."

George Bernard Shaw

"There is a sufficiency in the world for man's need but not for man's greed."

Mahatma Gandhi

"To the world you may be just one person, but to one person you may be the world."

Brandi Snyder

"The history of the world is the history of a few people who had faith in themselves."

Swami Vivekananda

"Everyone thinks of changing the world, but no one thinks of changing himself."

Leo Tolstoy

"Be the change that you want to see in the world."

Mahatma Gandhi

"...the world has been made by fools that wise men should live in it."

Oscar Wilde

"The hardest thing to understand in the world is the income tax."

Albert Einstein

"A gentleman is one who puts more into the world than he takes out."

George Bernard Shaw

"The world is a dangerous place, not because of those who do evil, but because of those who look on and do nothing."

Albert Einstein

"Conquer yourself, and the whole universe is yours."

Swami Vivekananda

"The world is preparing for a big change. Will you help?"

Sri Aurobindo Ghosh

"In a gentle way, you can shake the world."

Mahatma Gandhi

"Your life is your message to the world. Make sure it's inspiring."

Eknath Easwaran

"The world is a book, and those who do not travel read only a page."

Saint Augustine

"I want to put a ding in the universe."

Steve Jobs

"Spiritual emptiness is a universal disease."

Rick Warren

"The world has never been a paradise to live in nor will it ever be so."

Radha Swami

"Service to society is the rent we pay for living on this planet."

Joseph Murray

"If you want to kill an idea in this world, get a committee working on it."

Charles Kettering

"Making the ungrateful in the world grateful, is one of the most difficult tasks."

Ashok Sawhney

32

Society, Youth, Men, Women and People

"If you want something said, ask a man . . . if you want something done, ask a woman."

Margaret Thatcher

"You can fool all the people some of the time, and some of the people all the time, but you cannot fool all the people all the time."

Abraham Lincoln

"Woman, in your laughter you have the music of the fountain of life."

Rabindranath Tagore

"What is better than wisdom? Woman. And what is better than a good woman? Nothing."

Geoffrey Chaucer

"Women are born worshippers."

Thomas Carlyle

"God made the woman for the man and for the good and increase of the world."

Alfred Lord Tennyson

"With women the heart argues, not the mind."

Matthew Arnold

"'Tis woman, woman, rules us still."

Thomas Moore

"There are basically two types of people. People who accomplish things, and people who claim to have accomplished things. The first group is less crowded."

Mark Twain

"Women read men more truly than men read women."

Charlotte Bronte

"There are only two levers which can drive men - fear and interest."

Napoleon Bonapart

"Man is not the creature of circumstances. Circumstances are the creatures of man."

Benjamin Disraeli

"Being born in a stable, does not make a man a horse."

Arthur Wellesley

"It is the common wonder of all men, how among so many millions of faces, there should be none alike."

Thomas Brown

"Crowd psychology is a blind force."

Rabindranath Tagore

"Whatever the mind of man can conceive and believe, it can achieve."

Napoleon Hill

"Lawyers are always more ready to get a man into troubles, than out of them."

Oliver Goldsmith

"From woman is man born, inside her he is conceived. From woman originate new generations - why abuse her of whom are born great ones of the earth."

Adi Granth

"Some people come in life as blessings. Some come in your life as lessons."

Mother Teresa

"Crying is for plain women. Pretty women go shopping."

Oscar Wilde

"A race horse is an animal that can take several thousand people for a ride at the same time."

Marjorie Johnson

"Santa Claus has the right idea. Visit people once a year."

Victor Borge

"A pessimist is a man who thinks all women are bad; an optimist is one who hopes they are."

Chauncey Depew

"A man never tells you anything until you contradict him."

George Bernard Shaw

"You can tell whether a man is clever by his answers. You can tell whether a man is wise by his questions."

Naquib Mahfouz

"A committee is a group of people who individually can do nothing, but together can decide that nothing can be done."

Fred Allen

"A man can be happy with any woman, as long as he does not love her."

Oscar Wilde

"None are so fond of secrets as those who do not mean to keep them."

C.C. Colton

"The test of a man or woman's breeding is how they behave in a quarrel."

George Bernard Shaw

"The spaces between your fingers were created so that another's could fill them in."

Asa Butterfield

"Never forget 3 types of people in your life:
1. Who helped you in your difficult times.
2. Who left you in your difficult times.
3. Who put you in difficult times."

Anonymous

"With stones you can build walls to separate people or build bridges to unite them."

Mehmet Murat Ildan

"Fools admire, but men of sense approve."

Alexander Pope

"The minority is sometimes right; the majority always wrong."

George Bernard Shaw

"Beware the fury of a patient man."

John Dryden

"A man should never be ashamed to own he had been in the wrong, which is but saying, in other words, that he is wiser today than he was yesterday."

Jonathan Swift

"The madman who knows that he is mad, is close to sanity."

Ruiz De Alarcon

"Everything comes, if a man only waits."

Benjamin Disraeli

"Women are never disarmed by compliments. Men always are. That is the difference between the sexes."

Oscar Wilde

"I keep six honest serving men. (They taught me all I knew); Their names are What and Why and When and Now and Where and Who."

Rudyard Kipling

"Those who differ upon reason may come together by reason."

Benjamin Whichcote

"If one plays good music people don't listen, and if one plays bad music people don't talk."

Oscar Wilde

"Men are always sincere. They change sincerities, that's all."

Tristan Bernard

"A man who wants to do something will find a way; a man who doesn't will find an excuse."

Stephen Dolley

"He who knows not and knows not; he knows not: is a fool: shun him
He who knows not and knows he knows not; he is simple: teach him.
He who knows but knows not that he knows; he is asleep: wake him.
He who knows and knows that he knows, he is wise: follow him."

Confucius

"Mobile phones are the only subject on which men boast about who's got the smallest."

Neil Kinnock

"The hope of the world is the man who keeps right on, changing his methods if he must, but not his purpose."

Herbert Casson

"A boss who makes his men realize they have more ability than they think they have, will find they consistently do better work than they thought they could."

J.K. Lagemann

"Remember that a man's name is to him the sweetest sound in the English language, so if you can remember it, you will be trailing clouds of glory."

Dale Carnegie

"Responsibilities gravitate to the person who can shoulder them; power flows to the man who knows how."

Elbert Hubbard

"The public have an insatiable curiosity to know everything, except what is worth knowing.

Oscar Wilde

"Look in the face of the person to whom you are speaking if you wish to know his real sentiments; for he can command his words more easily than his countenance."

Lord Chesterfield

"A man of stature has no need of status."

Charles H. Brower

"A person must come to the point of thinking big about everything. Really, the secret of life is to think big, believe big, pray big, act big, and big results will come."

Dr. Norman Vincent Peale

"One should choose for a wife only such a woman, as he would choose for a friend, were she a man."

Joubert

"The only way for a rich man to be healthy is, by exercise and abstinence, to live as if he were poor."

Dr. Paul D. White

"The youth of a nation are the trustees of posterity."

Benjamin Disraeli

"Clever and attractive women do not want to vote; they are willing to let men govern as long as they govern men."

George Bernard Shaw

"He that cannot forgive others breaks the bridge over which he must pass himself, for every man has need to be forgiven."

George Herbert

"Only dull people are brilliant at breakfast."

Oscar Wilde

"When a woman is talking to you, listen to what she says with her eyes."

Victor Hugo

"What you do not want done to yourself, do not do to others."

Confucius

"They may forget what you said, but they will never forget how you made them feel."

Carl W. Buechner

"The royal road to a man's heart is to talk to him about the things he treasures most."

Dale Carnegie

"A graceful and pleasing figure is a perpetual letter of recommendation."

Francis Bacon

"Women will never be as men because they have no wives to advise them."

Dick Van Dyke

"A great revolution is never the fault of the people, but of the government."

Johann Wolfgang Von Goethe

"A sudden bold and unexpected question doth many times surprise a man and lay him open."

Francis Bacon

"A person who never made a mistake never tried anything new."

Albert Einstein

"Too many people are looking for the right person, instead of being the right person."

Corrina Bunch

"The moment there is suspicion about a person's motives, everything he does becomes tainted."

Mahatma Gandhi

"When a soldier kills his enemy, he is called a hero,
when a civilian kills a man, he is called a murderer."

Ashok Sawhney

"Wall Street is the only place that people drive to in a Rolls Royce, to take advice from those who use the subway."

Warren Buffet

"The best 3 methods of mass communication are telephone, television and tell-a-woman."

Board of Wisdom

"People laugh at me because I am different; I laugh at them because they are all the same."

Swami Vivekananda

"People who think they know everything are a great annoyance to those of us who do."

Issac Asimou

"There are two theories to argue with women:
1. If she is right then be fair to her and keep quiet,
2. If she is wrong, be kind to yourself and keep quiet."

Will Rogers

"No man has a good enough memory to be a successful liar."

Abraham Lincoln

"A human being is worse than any beast, when he turns into a beast."

Rabindranath Tagore

"The happiest people don't necessarily have the best of everything; they just make the most of everything that comes their way."

Louis G. Morton

"The dog is a gentleman. I hope to go to his heaven, not man's."

Mark Twain

"An expert is a man who has stopped thinking - 'he knows.'"

Frank Lloyd

"The cynic knows the price of everything and the value of nothing."

Oscar Wilde

"The things most people want to know about are usually, none of their business."

George Bernard Shaw

"The successful man is the one who had the chance and took it."

Roger Babson

"It is far better to be alone, than to be in bad company."

George Washington

"People often say that motivation doesn't last. Well, neither does bathing. That's why we recommend it daily."

Zig Ziglar

"If there were no bad people, there would be no good lawyers."

Charles Dickens

"That government is best which governs the least, because people discipline themselves."

Henry Thoreau

"All people want is someone to listen."

H. Eliot

"No man grows roses and cabbages for himself alone. You have to share to enjoy."

Chester Charles

"So long as men worship the Caesars and Napoleons, Caesars and Napoleons will duly rise and make them miserable."

Aldous Leonard

"No man was ever great by imitation."

Samuel Johnson

"We would all be idle if we could."

Samuel Johnson

"When you speak to a man, look in his eyes; when he speaks to you, look on his mouth."

Benjamin Franklin

"Best men are moulded out of faults."

William Shakespeare

"Man does not live by bread alone, but by faith, by admiration, by sympathy."

Ralph Waldo Emerson

"I hate mankind, for I think myself one of the best of them, and I know how bad I am."

Samuel Johnson

"Man everywhere is the born enemy of lies."

Thomas Carlyle

"It is one thing to show a man that he is in error, and another to put him in possession of truth."

John Locke

"Every woman deserves a man that can make her forget her heart was ever broken."

Elizabeth Gilbert

"I cannot choose the best. The best chooses me."

Rabindranath Tagore

"The worst distance between two people is misunderstanding."

Eva Marks

"The apparel oft proclaims the man."

William Shakespeare

"Elections are won by men and women chiefly because most people vote against somebody, rather than for somebody."

Franklin Pierce Adams

"A committee is a group that keeps minutes and loses hours."

Milton Berle

"People won't have time for you if you are always angry or complaining."

Stephen Hawking

"Treat people as if they were what they ought to be and you will help them become what they are capable of becoming."

Johann Wolfgang Von Goethe

"Everyone is prepared to reform others, but not themselves."

Ashok Sawhney

33

Prayer, Worship and Poetry

"Let me not pray to be sheltered from dangers, but to be fearless in facing them. Let me not beg for the stilling of my pain, but for the heart to conquer it. Let me not crave in anxious fear to be saved, but hope for the patience to win my freedom. Grant me that I may not be a coward, feeling your mercy in my success alone; but let me find the grasp of your hand in my failure."

Rabindranath Tagore

"What did you gain by prayer? I gained nothing. In fact, I lost anger, depression, jealousy, irritation & insecurity!"

Swami Vivekanand

"Prayer is the contemplation of the facts of life from the highest point of view."

Ralph Waldo Emerson

"More things are wrought by prayer than this world dreams of."

Alfred Lord Tennyson

"Pray but don't demand . Your desires may be less but God might be willing to give you more."

Ashok Sawhney

"Who rises from prayer a better man, his prayer is answered."

George Meredith

"If radio's slim fingers can pluck a melody
From night and toss it over a continent or sea;
If the petalled white notes of violin
Are blown across the mountains or the city's din;
If songs, like crimson roses, are culled from thin blue air-
Why should mortals wonder if God hears prayer?"

Ethel Romig Fuller

"Pray till prayer makes you forget your own wish, and leave it or merge it in God's will."

Frederick W. Robertson

"Prayer must never be answered: if it is, it ceases to be prayer and becomes correspondence."

Oscar Wilde

"It matters not how oft you kneel in attitude of prayer so true,
unless inside, where no man sees, your very soul is kneeling too."

Mary L. O'hara

"Thank you God, is the best prayer in life."

Ashok Sawhney

"There are times in a man's life when, regardless of the attitude of the body, the soul is on its kneels in prayer."

Victor Hugo

"O God, grant us the serenity to accept
What cannot be changed;
The courage to change what can be changed;
And wisdom to know one from the other."

Swami Vivekananda

"Complaint is the largest tribute heaven receives."

Jonathan Swift

"Constant complaint is the poorest sort of pay, for all the comforts we enjoy."

Benjamin Franklin

"A praying heart is a grateful heart."

Ashok Sawhney

"Why do we close our eyes when we pray, cry, kiss, dream? Because the most beautiful things in life are not seen but felt only by heart!"

Denzel Washington

"A person who spends some time on his knees for prayer in front of God, will never find it difficult to stand on his feet throughout his life."

Richard Challoner

"Prayer is not an attempt to change God's mind, but it's an attempt to let God change our minds."

Eric Turner

"We turn to God for help when our foundations are shaking, only to realise that it is God who is shaking them."

Charles C. West

"A time for prayer.
In times of war and not before, God and the soldier we adore, but in times of peace and all things righted, God is forgotten and soldier slighted."

Rudyard Kipling

"Many of our prayers were not answered and for this, we are now grateful."

William Feather

"To give pleasure to someone by a single act is better than a thousand hands bowing in prayer."

Mahatma Gandhi

"Laughter is a prayer. If you can laugh, you have learnt how to pray."

Osho

"Pray but don't demand. Your desires may be less but God might be willing to give you more."

Ashok Sawhney

"Pray as though everything depended on God. Work as though everything depended on you."

St. Augustine

"To pray is to let go and let God take over."

Philippians

"As civilizations advance, poetry almost necessarily declines."

Thomas B. Macaulay

"My secret is simple: I pray."

Mother Teresa

"May we pray for a return to God . . . and morals in our country."

Jim Bowser

"The power of prayer is indescribable, its glory is ineffable. Sincere devotees only realise its usefulness and splendor."

Ashok Sawhney

34

God, Lord and Devil

"God is an invisible parent, and parents are visibles gods. If you love and take care of the visible God, the invisible parent will definitely take care of you."

Daxini Nirav

"When God takes away something from your hands don't think he's punishing you. He's just leaving you empty handed to receive something better...."

The Bible

"I'm an atheist and I thank God for it."

George Bernard Shaw

"His own mornings are new surprises to God."

Rabindranath Tagore

"The nature of God is a circle whose center is everywhere and whose circumference is nowhere."

St. Augustine

"God says to us; you do what you like, but what happens is what I like; now you do what I like and what will happen, is what you like."

Ashok Sawhney

"To those who know thee not, no words can paint. And those who know thee, all words are faint."

Hannah More

"I fear one day I'll meet God. He'll sneeze and I won't know what to say."

Ronnie Shakes

"God is in your heart. Search him within. If you don't find Him there, you will not find Him anywhere."

Ashok Sawhney

"All men are born with a nose and ten fingers, but no one was born with a knowledge of God."

Voltaire

"I am sure God keeps no one waiting unless he sees that it is good for him to wait."

C.S. Lewis

"If you want to make God laugh, tell him about your plans."

Woody Allen

"God isn't an option, he's a necessity."

Janet Dick

"God seeks comrades and claims love, the devil seeks slaves and claims obedience."

Rabindranath Tagore

"It is sad. One half of the world does not believe in God, and the other half does not believe in me."

Oscar Wilde

"Rebellion to tyrants is obedience to God."

Benjamin Franklin

"No man has a right to expect blessings from God if he through greed and covetousness blocks the pathway down which God's blessings march."

Andy Zubko

"We must not miss any occasion whatsoever, to glorify God."

Ashok Sawhney

"There are people in the world so hungry, that God cannot appear to them except in the form of bread."

Mahatma Gandhi

"When the solution is simple, God is answering."

Albert Einstein

"Coincidence is God's way of remaining anonymous."

Albert Einstein

"To love another person is to see the face of God."

Victor Hugo

"God has not promised skies always blue, flower-strewn pathways all our life through; God has not promised sun without rain, joy without sorrow, peace without pain."

A.P.J. Abdul Kalam

"By being grateful to God, you live in continuous affluence."

Ashok Sawhney

"You don't choose your family. They are God's gift to you, as you are to them."

Desmond Tutu

"When men destroy their old Gods, they will find new ones to take their place."

Pearl S. Buck

"Suicide is man's way of telling God,
'You can't fire me - I quit.'"

Bill Matter

"Develop an attitude of gratitude, remembering that whatever is happening is because of God's blessings on you."

Ashok Sawhney

"To be closer to God, be closer to people."

Khalil Gibran

"You cannot believe in God until you believe in yourself."

Swami Vivekananda

"Better than worshiping Gods is obedience to the laws of righteousness."

Buddha

"All existence is a manifestation of God."

Sri Aurobindo Ghosh

"God has put something noble and good into every heart his hand created."

Mark Twain

"Give God your weakness and he'll give you his strength."

The Bible

"God has a special timing: never early, never late. It takes a little patience and faith but it's worth the wait."

Quran

"God loves each of us as if there was only one of us."

St. Augustine

"Try first thyself and after call God; for to the worker, God himself lends aid."

Euripides

"God has given us a gift of 10800 breaths a day. Use some to say 'Thank You God.'"

Ashok Sawhney

"God judged it better to bring good out of evil, than to suffer no evil to exist."

St. Augustine

"Meditation is shifting your attention to the part of yourself that is already connected to God."

John Gray

"He, who has no need for society, must be either a beast or God."

Aristotle

"If God did not exist, it would be necessary to invent him."

Voltaire

"I sometimes think that God in creating man, somewhat over-estimated his ability."

Oscar Wilde

"Put God first and you'll never be last."

The Bible

"Theist and atheist: the fight between them is as to whether God shall be called God or shall have some other name."

Samuel Butler

"Danger past, God is forgotten."

Thomas Fuller

"When we put our problems in God's hands, he puts his peace in our hearts."

Joe Stowell

"Life was never meant to be lived without God."

Solaced Oasis

"As long as you know that God is for you, it doesn't matter who is against you."

The Bible

"When God delays, he always delays for a greater purpose."

Tony Evans

"Consider the fact that maybe God closed that door because he knew you were worth so much more."

Allison Elsasser

"Feel that God works through your hands, sees through your eyes and hears through your ears."

Ashok Sawhney

35

Thankfulness and Gratitude

"He who receives a benefit with gratitude, prepays the first installment on his debt."

Seneca

"Gratitude is a vaccine, an antitoxin, and an antiseptic."

John Henry Jowett

"I have too many flaws to be perfect, but I have too many blessings to be ungrateful."

Zig Ziglar

"The goal of human life is God realisation."

Sri Ramakrishna Parmhans

"It is not happy people who are thankful. It is thankful people who are happy."

Anonymous

"Some people grumble that roses have thorns; I am grateful that thorns have roses."

Alphonse Karr

"We must find time to stop and thank the people who make a difference in our lives."

John F. Kennedy

"We should certainly count our blessings, but we should also make our blessings count."

Neal A. Maxwell

"Lukewarm acceptance is much more bewildering than outright rejection."

Martin Luther King

"What separates privilege from entitlement, is gratitude."

Brene Brown

"They do not love, that do not show their love."

William Shakespeare

"Gratitude is an overflow of the pleasure that fills your heart and soul."

Ashok Sawhney

"Never in the field of human conflict was so much owed by so many to so few."

Winston S. Churchill

"When I started counting my blessings, my whole life turned around."

Willie Nelson

"The person, whom you favored with a loan if he be a good man, will think himself in your debt ever after he has paid you."

Richard Steel

"An attitude of gratitude solves everything."

Ashok Sawhney

36

Yesterday, Today and Tomorrow

"We live on a moving line between past and future. That line is our lifeline."

George A. Buttrick

"There is no distance on this earth as far away as yesterday."

Robert Nethan

"Yesterday is a history. Tomorrow is a mystery. Today is a gift, that's why we call it the present."

Babatunde Olatunji

"Keep your words soft and tender, tomorrow, you may have to eat them."

Anonymous

"Don't count the days, make the days count."

Amy Rees Anderson

"Yesterday is a cancelled cheque, tomorrow is a promissory note. Today is cash on the line."

Hank Stram

"Worry never robs tomorrow of its sorrow. It only saps today of its joy."

Leo Buscaglia

"I am not afraid of tomorrow, for I have seen yesterday and I love today."

William Allen White

"Remember, today is the tomorrow you worried about yesterday."

Dale Carnegie

"Either you run the day, or the day runs you."

Jim Rohn

"Everyday may not be good. But there is something good in everyday."

Alice Morse Earle

"Talk to yourself once in a day otherwise you may miss meeting an excellent person in this world."

Swami Vivekananda

"Give every day the chance to become the most beautiful of your life."

Mark Twain

"The best preparation for tomorrow is doing your best today."

H. Jackson Brown Jr.

"Don't judge each day by the harvest you reap, but by the seeds that you plant."

Robert Louis Stevenson

"I don't know what tomorrow holds, but I know who holds tomorrow."

Jesse Jackson

"Today is the future I created yesterday."

Louise Hay

"Every morning we are born again. What we do today is what matters most."

Anonymous

"Live your life as if today is the first day of the rest of your life."

Ashok Sawhney

37

Problems, Troubles and Solutions

"Worry is a thin stream of fear trickling through the mind. If encouraged, it cuts a channel into which all other thoughts are drained."

Arthur Somers Roche

"Nothing happens to anybody which he is not fitted by nature to bear."

Marcus Aurelius

"You will only be remembered for two things: the problems you solve or the ones you create."

Mike Murdock

"Problems in relationships occur, because each person is concentrating on what is missing in the other person."

Wayne Dyer

"Most people are about as happy, as they make up their minds to be."

Abraham Lincoln

"A matter that becomes clear ceases to concern us."

Friedrich Nietzsche

"We cannot solve our problems with the same thinking we used when we created them."

Albert Einstein

"An obstacle is often a stepping stone."

Prescott

"It's not that I'm so smart, it's just that I stay with problems longer."

Albert Einstein

"In a day, when you don't come across any problems – you can be sure that you are travelling on a wrong path."

Swami Vivekananda

"Never say 'God I've a big problem, instead say – hey problem I've a big God.'"

Philippines Proverb

"Keep all your troubles and worries in your pocket . . . but make sure that your pocket has a hole."

Robert Frost

"Every difficulty slurred over will be a ghost to disturb your repose later on."

Rabindranath Tagore

"I've had a lot of worries in my life, most of which never happened."

Mark Twain

"If a problem can be solved, there is no use worrying about it. If it cannot be solved worrying will do no good."

Dalai Lama

"Count your blessings, not your troubles."

Dale Carnegie

"Kites rise highest against the wind, not with it."

Winston Churchill

"The way I see it, if you want the rainbow, you've got to put up with the rain."

Dolly Parton

"Do not expect troubles as they have a tendency not to disappoint."

Napoleon Hill

"Looking and looking for an illness often actually produces illness."

Dr. D.J. Schwartz

"When in trouble, I remember God as a matter of habit."

Ashok Sawhney

38

Wisdom and Foolishness

"Wise men never wail their present woes. But presently prevent the ways to wail."

William Shakespeare

"The journey of thousand miles begins with one step."

Lao Tse

"Knowledge is proud that it knows so much; Wisdom is humble that it knows no more."

William Cowper

"A man may learn wisdom even from a foe."

Aristophanes

"The difference between stupidity and genius is that genius has its limits."

Albert Einstein

"If a blind man catches another blind man's stick, they both will fall into a pit."

Saint Tukaram

"Fools rush in where angels fear to tread."

Alexander Pope

"He that makes himself an ass must not take ill if men ride him."

Thomas Fuller

"The wise through excess of wisdom is made a fool."

Ralph Waldo Emerson

"Silence is the virtue of fools."

Francis Bacon

"If the fool would persist in his folly, he would become wise."

William Blake

"A learned blockhead is a greater blockhead than an ignorant one."

Benjamin Franklin

"The folly of one man is the fortune of another."

Francis Bacon

"The farther backward you can look, the farther forward you are likely to see."

Winston Churchill

"No man really becomes a fool, until he stops asking questions."

Charles P. Steinmetz

"I learned long ago, never to wrestle with a pig. You get dirty, and besides, the pig likes it."

George Bernard Shaw

"Let us be thankful for the fools. But for them the rest of us could not succeed."

Mark Twain

"My grandfather always said that living is like licking honey off a thorn."

Louis Adamic

"Most of the shadows of this life are caused by standing in one's own sunshine."

Ralph Waldo Emerson

"When a stupid man is doing something he is ashamed of, he always declares that it is his duty."

George Bernard Shaw

"It's easier to fool people than to convince them they have been fooled."

Mark Twain

"We cannot swing up a rope that is attached only to our own belt."

William Ernest Hocking

"The lowest ebb is the turn of the tide."

Henry Wadsworth Longfellow

"Storms make oaks take deeper root."

George Herbert

"Never argue with a fool. Onlookers may not be able to tell the difference."

Mark Twain

"Men are wise in proportion not to their experience but to their capacity for experience."

George Bernard Shaw

"Wise men talk because they have something to say. Fools talk because they have to say something."

Plato

"There are many things of which a wise man may wish to be ignorant."

Ralph Waldo Emerson

"After the event even the fool is wise."

P. Waterinckx

"The art of being wise, is the art of knowing, what to overlook."

William James

"A prudent question is one half of wisdom."

Francis Bacon

"I am patient with stupidity, but not with those who are proud of it."

E. Sitwell

"Many receive advice, few profit by it."

Publilius Syrus

"When intelligence speaks, wisdom listens."

Socrates

"If you can't explain it simply, you don't understand it well enough."

Albert Einstein

"It is better to keep your mouth closed and let people think you are a fool than to open it and remove all doubt."

Mark Twain

"Wisdom is not a product of schooling but of the lifelong attempt to acquire it."

Albert Einstein

"The highest wisdom is sometimes found in the lowest people."

Matshona Dhliwayo

"Talk sense to a fool and he calls you foolish."

Euripides

"We must never argue with an ignorant man, as it is impossible to defeat him."

Ashok Sawhney

"The greatest lesson in life is to know that even fools are right sometimes."

Winston Churchill

"The wisdom of life consists in elimination of non essentials."

Humayum Toba

"Learn from the mistakes of others. You can't live long enough to make them all yourself."

Eleanor Roosevelt

"Wisdom is knowing when to speak your mind and when to mind your speech."

Evangel

"There is a crack in everything, that's how the light gets in."

Leonard Cohen

"If you stand with a lantern it may light up your path for 10 meters, but if you start walking with it, it will illuminate your path for miles together."

Ashok Sawhney

39

Work, Action and Practice

"Errors like straws upon the surface flow, who would search for pearls to be grateful for often must dive below."

John Dryden

"There is nothing truly valuable which can be purchased without pains and labour."

Thomas A. Edison

"All the beautiful sentiments in the world weigh less than a single lovely action."

James Russell Lowell

"Blessed is he who was has found his work; let him ask no other blessedness."

Thomas Carly

"Work, ever performing work, is the first principle of success."

Swami Ramtirtha

"Love what you do, do what you love."

Ray Bradbury

"All that is essential for the triumph of evil is that good men do nothing."

Edmund Burke

"The reward of a thing well done, is to have done it."

Ralph Waldo Emerson

"Laziness is your biggest enemy."

Jawaharlal Nehru

"Nothing is so good as it seems beforehand."

George Eliot

"Great acts are made up of small deeds."

Lao Tzu

"God gives every bird its food, but does not throw it into the nest."

J.G. Holland

"Action is the foundational key to all success."

Pablo Picasso

"The secret of being miserable is to have leisure to bother about whether you are happy or not. The cure for it is occupation."

George Bernard Shaw

"Take time to deliberate; but when the time for action arrives, stop thinking and go in."

Napoleon Bonaparte

"Action may not always bring happiness; but there is no happiness without action."

Benjamin Disraeli

"If a man does his best, what else is there."

Gen. S. Patton

"Small deeds done are better than great deeds planned."

Peter Marshall

"Do the most uninteresting tasks first, the pleasanter ones last."

J.D. Ratcliff

"A jug fills drop by drop."

Buddha

"An ounce of practice is worth more than tons of preaching."

Mahatma Gandhi

"If you can't fly, then run, If you can't run, then walk, If you can't walk, then crawl, but whatever you do, you have to keep moving forward."

Martin Luther King, Jr.

"Whatever you do will be insignificant, but it is very important that you do it."

Mahatma Gandhi

"The highest reward for man's toil is, not what he gets for it, but what he becomes by it."

John Ruskin

"Be not solitary, be not idle."

Robert Burton

"Have thy tools ready. God will find thee work."

Charles Kingsley

"Executive ability is deciding quickly and getting somebody else to do the work."

Earl Nightingale

"If you get a kick out of your job, others will get a kick out of working for you."

Charles H. Brower

"Do not let what you cannot do interfere with what you can do."

John Wooden

"Insanity: doing the same thing over and over again and expecting different results."

Albert Einstein

"A job is what we do for money, work is what we do for love."

Marysarah Quinn

"Work spares us from three evils; boredom, vice, need."

Voltaire

"Do one thing at a time, and while doing it put your whole soul into it to the exclusion of all else."

Swami Vivekananda

"A successful man is one who can lay a firm foundation with the bricks others have thrown at him!"

David Brinkley

"By failing to prepare, you are preparing to fail."

Benjamin Franklin

"Work like a horse and live like a hermit."

Legal Trigger

"You can't cross the sea merely by standing and staring at the water."

Rabindranath Tagore

"Those who do not read the news are un-informed. Those that do are mis-informed."

Mark Twain

"Nothing worth having, comes easy."

Theodore Roosevelt

"Constant dripping hollows out a stone."

Lucretius

"Continuous effort – not strength or intelligence – is the key to unlocking our potential."

Helen Keller

"It always seems impossible until it's done."

Nelson Mandela

"Iron rusts from disuse; water loses its purity from stagnation . . . even so does inaction sap the vigor of the mind."

Leonardo da Vinci

"I never see what has been done; I only see what remains to be done."

Buddha

"You cannot plough a field by turning it over in your mind."

Gordon B. Hinckley

"It is not only for what we do, but also what we do not do, for which we are accountable."

Moliere

"Well done is better than well said."

Benjamin Franklin

"Change doesn't come in nickels and dimes. It comes in dedication and sweat."

Toni Sorenson

"If you can't outplay them, outwork them."

Ben Hogan

"I will go anywhere as long as it is forward."

David Livingston

"A pint of sweat saves a gallon of blood."

George S. Patton

"Even if you're on the right track, you'll get run over if you just sit there."

Will Rogers

"When your work speaks for itself, don't interrupt."

Henry J. Kaiser

"It does not matter how slowly you go as long as you do not stop."

Confucius

"The only way to do great work is to love what you do."

Steve Jobs

"Laziness is nothing more than the habit of resting before you get tired."

Jules Renard

"Nobody can think straight who does not work. Idleness wraps the mind."

Henry Ford

"Excellence in any department can be attained only by labour of a lifetime; it is not to be purchased at a lesser price."

Dr. Samuel Johnson

"Nothing great was ever achieved without enthusiasm."

Ralph Waldo Emerson

"Suit the action to the word, the word to the action."

William Shakespeare

"Right action is the end of all knowledge and all meditation."

Chakarvati Rajgopalacharya

"Action is eloquence."

William Shakespeare

"Our deeds determine us, as much as we determine our deeds."

Charge Elyot

"Great thoughts reduced to practice become great acts."

William Hazlitt

"Deeds, not words, shall speak me."

John Fletcher

"The words are lovely, dark and deep,
But I have promises to keep,
And miles to go before I sleep,
And miles to go before I sleep."

Ralph Waldo Emerson

"Woods are lovely, dark and deep but I have promises to keep, miles to go before I sleep and miles to go before I sleep."

Robert Frost

"I have nothing to offer but blood, toil, tears and sweat."

Winston Churchill

"The actions of men are the best interpreters of their thoughts."

John Locke

"I walk slowly, but I never walk backward."

Abraham Lincoln

"Strong reasons make strong actions."

William Shakespeare

"We put our love where we have put our labour."

Ralph Waldo Emerson

"No race can prosper till it learns there is as much dignity in tilling a field, as in writing a poem."

Booker T. Washington

"If you want to learn about team work, play hockey."

Ashok Sawhney

40

Justice and Punishment

"Justice must be done, but it mustn't be confused with revenge as they are not the same."

Ashok Sawhney

"Justice delayed is justice denied."

William E. Gladstone

"Justice without force is powerless, force without justice is tyrannical."

Blaise Pascal

"Justice that love gives is a surrender, justice that law gives is a punishment."

Mahatma Gandhi

"A fine is a tax for doing wrong, a tax is a fine for doing well."

Mark Twain

"The liar's punishment is not in the least that he is not believed, but that he cannot believe anyone else."

George Bernard Shaw

"Where justice is destroyed by injustice, or truth by falsehood, while the judges look on, there they shall also be destroyed."

Manusmriti

"Those who judge will never understand, and those who understand will never judge."

Wilson Kanadi

"I think the first duty of society is justice."

Alexander Hamilton

"Punishment is justice for the unjust."

St. Augustine

"We win justice quickest by rendering justice to the other party."

Mahatma Gandhi

"Too often we judge other groups by their worst examples, while judging ourselves by our best intentions."

George W. Bush

"The moral arc of the universe is long, but it bends toward justice."

Martin Luther King

"When justice is done, it brings joy to the righteous but terror to evildoers."

Proverbs

"By forgiving another, I am trusting that God is a better justice-maker than I am."

Jamie Georqe

"What we have in us of the image of God, is the love of truth and justice."

Demosthenes

"Justice is conscience, not a personal conscience but the conscience of the whole of humanity."

Aleksandr Solzhenitsyn

"It is better to risk saving a guilty person than to condemn an innocent one."

Voltaire, Zadig

"It is reasonable that everyone who asks justice should do justice."

Thomas Jefferson

"Harsh justice is still justice."

George RR Martin

"The rape of justice anywhere, violates justice everywhere."

Colin Tegerdine

"Who can protest an injustice but does not, is an accomplice to the act."

Talmud

"Don't mistake law for justice."

Charles T. Sprading

"Justice is my being allowed to do whatever I like. Injustice is whatever prevents my doing so."

Samuel Johnson

"Freedom for the wolves has often meant death to the sheep."

Isaiah Berlin

"Justice will prevail!"

Tsugumi Ohba

"A unjust law, is no law at all."

Martin Luther King Jr.

"As per my own experience, I found that sometimes, mercy produces richer fruits, than severe justice."

Ashok Sawhney

41

Knowledge and Ignorance

"Knowledge can only be got in one way, the way of experience. There is no other way to know."

Swami Vivekananda

"Beware of false knowledge; it is more dangerous than ignorance."

George Bernard Shaw

"Knowledge itself is power."

Francis Bacon

"Eloquence is the child of knowledge."

Benjamin Disraeli

"Knowledge is the antidote to fear."

Ralph Waldo Emerson

"Knowledge is of no value unless you put it into practice."

Anton Chekhov

"Everyone you will ever meet knows something you don't."

Bill Nye

"What we want is to see the child in pursuit of knowledge, and not knowledge in pursuit of the child."

George Bernard Shaw

"I like to listen. I have learned a great deal from listening carefully. Most people never listen."

Ernest Hemingway

"He who knows best, knows how little he knows."

Thomas Jefferson

"Fire in a piece of flint, knowledge exists in the mind. Suggestion is the friction which brings it out."

Swami Vivekananda

"To know everything about oneself, one must know all about others."

Oscar Wilde

"We can say of Shakespeare, that never has a man turned so little knowledge to such great account."

T.S. Eliot

"True knowledge is not attained by thinking. It is what you are; it is what you become."

Sri Aurobindo Ghosh

"An investment in knowledge pays the best interest."

Benjamin Franklin

"A good decision is based on knowledge, and not on numbers."

Plato

"Never confuse belief with knowledge."

Abhijit Naskar

"Knowledge is a tenant in the house of wisdom."

Matshona Dhliwayo

"Self-knowledge is the greatest kind of knowledge."

Abhijit Naskar

"There is no wealth like knowledge, and no poverty like ignorance."

Buddha

"Where ignorance is our master, there is no possibility of real peace."

Dalai Lama

"The greater our knowledge increases, the greater our ignorance unfolds."

John F. Kennedy

"Knowledge becomes evil, if the aim be not virtuous."

Plato

"Knowledge of what is, does not open the door directly to what should be."

Albert Einstein

"Knowledge is a treasure, but practice is the key to it."

Thomas Fuller

"There are only two kinds of people who are really fascinating-people who know absolutely everything, and people who know absolutely nothing."

Oscar Wilde

"The greater the knowledge, the greater the doubt."

Johann Wolfgang Von Goethe

"Knowledge like timber shouldn't be much used till they are seasoned."

Oliver Wendell Holmes

"Teach thy tongue to say, 'I do not know,' and thou shalt progress."

Maimonides

"Be lions roaring through the forests of knowledge."

Bahai Scriptures

"Imagination is more important than knowledge."

Albert Einstein

"You can't use up creativity. The more you use, the more you have."

Maya Angelou

"There are lights everywhere except in the minds of men."

Herbert Read

"That man who has followed any kind of knowledge to its highest points is a Rishi."

Sister Nivedita

"Ignorance is not innocence but sin."

Robert Browning

"Information is not knowledge."

Albert Einstein

"Not your loud voice but your approach, attitude and knowledge would force others to listen to you."

Ashok Sawhney

42

Marriage and Divorce

"Marriage has many pains, but celibacy has no pleasures."

Samuel Johnson

"Marriage is the perfection which love aimed at, ignorant of what is sought."

Ralph Waldo Emerson

"One fool at least in every married couple."

Henry Fielding

"Though marriage makes man and wife one flesh, it leaves 'em still two fools."

William Congreve

"Marriage is the greatest educational institution on earth."

Channing Pollock

"Marriage is like life in this that it is a field of battle, and not a bed of roses."

Robert Louis Stevenson

"Marriage is one long conversation, checkered by disputes."

Robert Louis Stevenson

"Choose a wife rather by your ear than your eye."

Thomas Fuller

"Happiness in marriage is entirely a matter of chance."

Jane Austen

"Marriage is a great civilizer of the world."

Robert Hall

"Hanging and marriage, you know, go by destiny."

George Farquhar

"Well-married a man is winged, illmatched, he is shackled."

Henry Ward Beecher

"Never marry but for love; but see that thou lovest what is lovely."

William Penn

"Married in haste, we repent at leisure."

William Congreve

"It is a woman's business to get married as soon as possible, and a man's to keep unmarried as long as he can."

George Bernard Shaw

"Both marriage and death ought to be welcome,
the one promises happiness, doubtless the other assures it."

Mark Twain

"Marriage is a bribe to make a housekeeper think she's a householder."

Thornton Wilder

"One was never married, and that's his hell; another is, and that's his plague."

Robert Burton

"In matrimony, to hesitate is sometimes to be saved."

Samuel Burton

"Though women are angels, yet wedlock's the devil."

Lord Byron

"Oh! How many torments lie in the small circle of a wedding-ring."

Colley Cibber

"In marriage do thou be wise; prefer the person before money, virtue before beauty, the mind before the body; then thou hast a wife, a friend, a companion, a second self."

William Penn

"Marriage is a good deal like a circus, there is not as much in it as is represented in the advertising."

E.W. Howe

"It's a capital thing for a woman to wed but a shocking bad thing for a man."

Lucas

"Maidens! Why should you worry in choosing whom shall you marry? Choose whom you may, you will find you have got somebody else."

John Hay

"An ideal wife is any woman who has an ideal husband."

Booth Tarkington

"Keep your eyes wide open before marriage, half shut afterward."

Benjamin Franklin

"A man's best fortune, or his worst, is his wife."

Thomas Fuller

"There may be good, but there are not pleasant marriages."

La Rochefoucauld

"Wives are youngmen's mistresses, companions for middle age, and old men's nurses."

Francis Bacon

"Wifehood in India is not woman's central function. That is motherhood. As mother, an Indian woman is supreme."

Sister Nivedita

"Ultimately the bond of all companionship, whether in marriage or in friendship, is conversation."

Oscar Wilde

"They say all marriages are made in heaven, but so are thunder and lightning."

Clint Eastwood

"A good marriage would be between a blind wife and a deaf husband."

Michel de Montaigne

"It is most unwise for people in love to marry."

George Bernard Shaw

"The word 'mother' is the endless shore on which all Indian souls find harbour."

Sister Nivedita

"In every marriage more than a week old, there are grounds for divorce. The trick is to find, and continue to find, grounds for marriage."

Robert Anderson

"I married my wife for her looks, but not the ones she is giving me lately."

Digerati

"A happy marriage is the union of two good forgivers."

Ruth Bell Graham

"Marriage is an alliance entered into by a man who can't sleep with the window shut, and a woman who can't sleep with the window open."

George Bernard Shaw

"No man should have a secret from his wife. She invariably finds it out."

Oscar Wilde

"If you want to be happy with your husband, love him less and understand more! If you want to be happy with your wife, love her more and never try to understand her!"

Chanakya

"Happiest couples in the world never have the same 'nature', they just have the best 'understanding' of their 'difference'."

Marquis Beach

"The goal in marriage is not to think alike, but to think together."

Robert C. Dodds

"Marriage is the triumph of imagination over intelligence."

Oscar Wilde

"A successful marriage requires falling in love many times, always with the same person."

Mignon McLaughlin

"I haven't spoken to my wife in years, I didn't want to interrupt her."

Rodney Dangerfield

"A wedding is just like a funeral except that you get to smell your own flowers."

Grace Hansen

"To keep your marriage brimming with love in the wedding cup, whenever you are wrong, admit it; whenever you are right, shut up."

Ogden Nash

"It's better to wait long . . . than marry wrong."

Brandon Shanks

"In a marriage, for their own personal happiness, both the partners are equally responsible."

Ashok Sawhney

43

Revenge and Forgiveness

"In taking revenge a man is but equal to his enemy, but in passing it over he is his superior."

Francis Bacon

"It is often better not to see an insult than to avenge it."

Seneca

"An eye for eye only ends up making the whole world blind."

Mahatma Gandhi

"Beware of the man who does not return your blow: he neither forgives you nor allows you to forgive yourself."

George Bernard Shaw

"A man who contemplates revenge keeps his wounds green."

Francis Bacon

"The best revenge is massive success."

Frank Sinatra

"Forgiveness is the king of all actions."

Ashok Sawhney

"Always forgive your enemies. Nothing annoys them so much."

Oscar Wilde

"The weak can never forgive. Forgiveness is the attribute of the strong."

Mahatma Gandhi

"A lean compromise is better than a fat law-suit."

George Herbert

"When restraint and courtesy are added to strength, the latter becomes irresistible."

Mahatma Gandhi

"Forgive others, not because they deserve forgiveness, but because you deserve peace . . . ."

Jonathan Lockwood

"Live like a tree, giving, forgiving and free."

Debasish Mridha

"From the experience of my life, I got a formula to live –
to some I apologised and others I learnt to forgive."

Ashok Sawhney

"Before you embark on a journey of revenge, dig two graves."

Marcus Aurelius

"I can forgive but cannot forget is only another way of saying, I will not forgive."

Henry W. Beecher

"Forgiveness is a funny thing. It warms the heart but cools the sting."

William Arthur Ward

"Forgive, forget. Bear with the faults of others as you would have them bear with yours."

Philips Brooks

"The dust receives insult and in return offers her flowers."

Rabindranath Tagore

"It is easier to forgive an enemy than to forgive a friend."

William Blake

"I have always found that mercy bears richer fruits than strict justice."

Abraham Lincoln

"He who forgives, even when is fully capable of taking revenge, is a real merciful person."

Ashok Sawhney

44

Music

"Music expresses that which can not be said and on which it is impossible be silent."

Victor Hugo

"Music moves us, and we know not why."

Letitia Elizabeth Landon

"A good ear for music, and a taste for music are two very different things which are often confounded."

Fulke Greville

"Music is a friend of labour."

William Green

"Such sweet compulsion doth in music lie."

John Milton

"What passion can not music raise and quell?"

John Dryden

"Life would be very dull without music."

Ashok Sawhney

45

Honesty and Integrity

"Honest bread is very well - it's the butter that makes the temptation."

Douglas Jerrold

"Honesty is not only the best policy. It is rare enough today to make you pleasantly conspicuous."

Charles H. Brower

"Integrity without knowledge is weak and useless, and knowledge without integrity is dangerous and dreadful."

Samuel Johnson

"It is difficult, but not impossible, to conduct strictly honest business."

Mahatma Gandhi

"Being entirely honest with oneself is a good exercise."

Sigmund Freud

"I am afraid we must make the world honest, before we can honestly say to our children that honesty is the best policy."

George Bernard Shaw

"A few honest men are better than numbers."

Oliver Cromwell

"You will surely find your treasure wherever your heart is."

Ashok Sawhney

46

Silence, Solitude and Contentment

"He who does not understand your silence will probably not understand your words."

Elbert Hubbard

"Silence is the mother of truth."

Benjamin Disraeli

"Silence is one of the hardest arguments to refute."

Josh Billings

"Our lives begin to end the day we become silent about things that matter."

Martin Luther King Jr.

"Better to remain silent and be thought a fool than to speak out and remove all doubt."

Abraham Lincoln

"No speech ever uttered or utterable is worth comparison with silence."

Thomas Carlyle

"The right word may be effective, but no word was ever as effective, as a rightly timed pause."

Mark Twain

"Solitude: a good place to visit, but a poor place to stay."

Josh Billings

"A creation of importance can only be produced when its author isolates himself, it is a child of solitude."

Johann Wolfgang Von Goethe

"Silence is the most perfect expression of scorn."

George Bernard Shaw

"If obesity is a disease, it is the only one you can cure, by keeping your mouth shut."

Rick Berman

"Silence and smile are two powerful tools. Smile is the way to solve many problems. And silence is the way to avoid many problems."

Iris Johansen

"Be silent or say something which is better than silence."

Ashok Sawhney

"Silence is the best answer to anger."

Mahatma Gandhi

"If thou thinkest twice before thou speakest once, thou wilt speak twice the better for it."

William Penn

"Speech is of time, silence is of eternity."

Thomas Carlyle

"Sometimes it takes sadness to know what happiness is, noise to appreciate silence and absence to value presence."

Anonymous

"No sound in this world can be more louder than silence. If anyone can understand your silence, they can never misunderstand your words."

Grey Empires

"Choose silence of all virtues, for by it you hear other men's imperfections, and conceal your own."

George Bernard Shaw

"Deepest feelings are always felt in silence."

Rhonda Huston

"Do not let the behavior of others destroy your inner peace."

Dalai Lama

"Poor and content is rich and rich enough."

William Shakespeare

"The noblest mind the best contentment has."

Edmund Spenser

"Men of few words are the best men."

William Shakespeare

"Never miss a good chance to shut up."

Will Rogers

"Silence is a source of great strength."

Lao Tzu

"Silence isn't empty. It's full of answers."

Anonymous

Speak less but listen more.
"Say one, when you hear two, as God has given you tongue one, but ear two."

Ashok Sawhney

47

Sufferings, Comfort and Pain

"In misery it is a great comfort to have a companion."

John Lyly

"All things are difficult, before they are easy."

Thomas Fuller

"Comfort the afflicted, and afflict the comfortable."

Finley Peter Dunne

"Out of suffering have emerged the strongest souls; the most massive characters are seared with scars."

Khalil Gibran

"We delight in the beauty of the butterfly, but rarely admit the changes it has gone through to achieve that beauty."

Maya Angelou

"When you have purity in your heart for the love of God, sufferance or comfort will have an equal degree of gratitude."

Ashok Sawhney

48

Mind, Ideas and Thoughts

"Your mind is a garden. Your thoughts are the seeds. You can grow flowers or you can grow weeds."

Unknown

"Whatever the mind can conceive and believe the mind can achieve."

Napoleon Hill

"The impure mind of a human is hell and absence of harmony and worries are the tortures."

Ashok Sawhney

"None can destroy iron, but its own rust can. Likewise, none can destroy a person but its own mindset can."

Ratan Tata

"Better an ugly face than an ugly mind."

James Ellis

"One man that has a mind and knows it, can always beat ten men who haven't and don't."

George Bernard Shaw

"Every impulse that we strive to strangle broods in the mind and poisons us .... The only way to get rid of temptation is to yield to it."

Oscar Wilde

"If you're too open-minded; your brains will fall out."

Lawrence Ferlinghetti

"Thought feeds itself with its own words and grows."

Rabindranath Tagore

"There is nothing either good or bad, but thinking makes it so."

William Shakespeare

"Thought is often bolder than speech."

Benjamin Disraeli

"The actions of men are the best interpreters of their thoughts."

John Locke

"Your mind is for having ideas, not holding them."

David Allen

"You are going to change your mind a thousand times, that is a good thing. Only imbeciles never change their minds."

Adam Dachis

"My words fly up, my thoughts remain below. Words without thoughts, never to heaven go."

William Shakespeare

"What is uttered from the heart alone, will win the hearts of others to your own."

Johann Wolfgang Von Goethe

"A great person is one who affects the minds of their generation."

Benjamin Disraeli

"At times the sound of silence is more powerful than the spoken word."

Ashok Sawhney

"Alter the mind and you alter the man."

William James

"Live for an ideal and leave no place in the mind for anything else."

Swami Vivekananda

"To keep the body in good health is a duty . . . otherwise we shall not be able to keep our mind strong and clear."

Buddha

"It is the mark of an educated mind to entertain a thought, without accepting it."

Aristotle

"Always bear in mind that your own resolution to succeed is more important than any other."

Abraham Lincoln

"A woman's mind is cleaner than a man's; she changes it more often."

Oliver Herford

"Yoga is a skillful strategy to calm down the mind."

St. Vashishta

"Regular meditation is a priceless tool for the recovery and maintenance of health."

Dr. Brain Weiss

"The ten minute period before you sleep and the ten minute period after you wake up, are profoundly influential on your subconscious mind."

Yogi Raman

"Learning never exhausts the mind."

Leonardo da Vinci

"Educating the mind without educating the heart, is no education at all."

Aristotle

"The teachings that can enlighten our souls, are better than gems and jewellery."

Ashok Sawhney

49

Sin, Virtue and Spirituality

"'Sins can be destroyed by charity', as mentioned in the Gita, 'Yajna, charity and austerity are purifying to the wise.'"

Ashok Sawhney

"I drink to make other people more interesting."

Ernest Hemingway

"Some rise by sin, and some by virtue fall."

William Shakespeare

"The hand that gives, is more virtuous, than the hand that receives."

Ashok Sawhney

"Above all temples of brick and stone is the temple of the heart."

Sadhu Vaswani

"I am a man, more sinned against than sinning."

William Shakespeare

"Virtue is insufficient temptation."

George Bernard Shaw

"The difference between sin and virtue is easily felt but it is so minute that expressing it becomes arduous."

Ashok Sawhney

"Virtue consists, not in abstaining from vice, but in not desiring it."

George Bernard Shaw

"They do not sin at all
Who sin for love."

Oscar Wilde

"Few love to hear the sins they love to act."

William Shakespeare

"Stealing to eat isn't criminal – stealing for greed to be rich is."

Ashok Sawhney

"Starvation, and not sin, is the parent of modern crime."

Oscar Wilde

"The greatest sin is to think of yourself as weak."

Swami Vivekananda

"What have women who have not sinned to do with me, or I with them? We do not understand each other."

Oscar Wilde

"Prosperity doth best discover vice, but adversity doth best discover virtue."

Francis Bacon

"Nothing but beauty and wisdom deserve immortality."

Will Durant

"Gratitude is the parent of all virtues."

Ashok Sawhney

50

Politicians, Diplomacy, King and Government

"A diplomat is a person who can tell you to go to hell in such a way that you actually look forward to the trip."

Caskie Stinnet

"Politics come from 'poll' a Latin word meaning 'many': and 'tics' meaning 'blood sucking creatures.'"

Robin Williams

"Divide and rule, the politician cries; unite and lead, is watchword of the wise."

Johann Wolfgang Von Goethe

"Politics is perhaps the only profession for which no preparation is thought necessary."

Robert Louis Stevenson

"In politics, victory is never total."

Donald Freed

"The proper function of a government is to make it easy for the people to do good and difficult for them to do evil."

William Ewart Gladstone

"No government can be long secure without a formidable opposition."

Benjamin Disraeli

"Misrule is better than no rule, and an ill government, a bad government is better than none."

Oliver Cromwell

"Let us never negotiate out of fear. But let us never fear to negotiate."

John F. Kennedy

"A government that robs Peter to pay Paul can always depend on the support of Paul."

George Bernard Shaw

"Politicians neither love nor hate."

John Dryden

"Asking politicians to give up a source of money, is like asking Dracula to forsake blood."

Cal Thomas

"A coalition government is like a single hook bra. Some wonder what's holding it, while others are waiting for it to fall down and grab the opportunity with both the hands!"

Anonymous

"He knows nothing and thinks he knows everything. That points clearly to a political career."

George Bernard Shaw

"A politician is someone who promises a bridge even when there's no water."

Gregory David Roberts

"A good politician is quite unthinkable as an honest burglar."

H.L. Mencken

"Politics is war without bloodshed, while war is politics with bloodshed."

Mao Zedong

"He is asked to stand, he wants to sit, he is expected to lie."

Winston Churchill (on Definition of a Politician)

"A diplomat is a man who always remembers a woman's birthday but never remembers her age."

Robert Frost

"A politician is a politician. I have a deep and profound mistrust when it comes to most of them."

Ashok Sawhney

51

Present, Past and Future

"The best thing about the future is that it comes only one day at a time."

Abraham Lincoln

"Why doesn't the past decently bury itself instead of sitting and waiting to be admitted by the present?"

D.H. Lawrence

"We are made wise not by the recollection of our past, but by the responsibility for our future."

George Bernard Shaw

"There is only one real tragedy in a woman's life. The fact that her past is always her lover, and her future invariably her husband."

Oscar Wilde

"A weed is no more than a flower in disguise."

James Lowell

"It is the fashion to style the present moment an extraordinary crisis."

Benjamin Disraeli

"He that fears not the future, may enjoy the present."

Thomas Fuller

"You can never plan the future by past."

Edmund Burke

"When all else is lost, the future still remains."

Christian Nestell

"No man is rich enough to buy back his past."

Oscar Wilde

"Even God cannot change the past."

Agathon

"Forget the past, remember the lesson."

Mandy Hale

"Deeds of the past life are reflected in the present life. This is the reincarnation cycle."

Ashok Sawhney

52

Victory, Defeat, Freedom and Democracy

"Victory is sweetest when you've known defeat."

Malcolm S. Forbes

"Victory has a thousand fathers, but defeat is an orphan."

John F. Kennedy

"We gain freedom when we have paid the full price."

Rabindranath Tagore

"Freedom is never dear at any price. It is the breath of life. What would a man not pay for living?"

Mahatma Gandhi

"If the loser keeps his smile, the winner will lose the thrill of victory!"

Dale Carnegie

"A man is not finished when he is defeated. He is finished when he quits."

Richard Nixon

"I have a very strong belief that truth and true love win ultimately over evil and misfortune in this world."

Ashok Sawhney

53

Attitude and Simplicity

"Your attitude, not your aptitude, will determine your altitude."

Zig Ziglar

"If you can't explain it simply, you don't understand it well enough."

Albert Einstein

"Do your best and leave the rest to God."

Ashok Sawhney

"The art of enjoying every minute is to deal with only one minute at a time."

Dr. Hilary Worth

"Character is the result of two things – mental attitude and the way we spend our time."

Elbert Hubbard

"Only put off until tomorrow what you are willing to die having left undone."

Pablo Picasso

"There is nothing either good or bad but thinking makes it so."

William Shakespeare

"The only disability in life is a bad attitude."

Scott Hamilton

"Don't let what you cannot do interfere with what you can do."

John R. Wooden

"If you're going through hell, keep going."

Winston Churchill

"For success, attitude is equally as important as ability."

Harry F. Banks

"Success is largely a matter of holding on after others have let go."

William Feathers

"If I had eight hours to chop down a tree, I'd spend six hours sharpening my axe."

Abraham Lincoln

"I have the simplest tastes. I am always satisfied with the best."

Oscar Wilde

"We don't see things as they are, we see them as we are."

Anais Nin

"Between craft and credulity, the voice of reason is stifled."

Edmund Burke

"There is a certain majesty in simplicity which is far above all the quaintness of wit."

Alexander Pope

"Manifest plainness. Embrace simplicity."

Lao Tzu

"The whole life we make this mistake; our own face is full of dust, but we keep trying to clean the mirror."

Ashok Sawhney

"The treasure that is precious is the quality of even-mindedness in all situations."

Sri Sathya Sai Baba

"He is happy whose circumstances suit his temper; but he is excellent who suits his temper to any circumstances."

David Hume

"With stones you can build walls to separate people or build bridges to unite them."

Mehmet Murat Ildan

"Keep a secret, it is your slave. Tell it and it is your master."

Wilson Allen

"Little adjustment is always better than a lengthy argument."

Salman Mansuri

"I look only to the good qualities of men. Not being faultness myself, I won't presume to probe into the faults of others."

Mahatma Gandhi

"Even if you do not have natural talent, you can win with dedication and hard work."

Ashok Sawhney

"When it rains, look for rainbows. When it's dark look for stars."

Beeld Steil

"Never complain and never explain."

Benjamin Disraeli

"Softly speak and sweetly smile."

Thomas A. Edison

"It's not what happens to you, but how you react to it that matters."

Epictetus

"Everything is funny, as long as it's happening to somebody else."

Will Rogers

"When the going gets tough, the tough get going."

Joseph P. Kennedy

"Simplicity is the ultimate sophistication."

Leonardo da Vinci

"Happiness is a present attitude, not a future condition."

Hugh Prather

"Out of intense complexities intense simplicities emerge."

Winston Churchill

"Distrust that man who tells you to distrust."

Ella Wheeler Wilcox

"Be strong, but not rude; be kind, but not weak; be bold, but not bully; be humble, but not timid; be proud, but not arrogant."

Zig Ziglar

"There is no agony like bearing an untold story inside you."

Michelangelo

"It's not the load that breaks you down, it's the way you carry it."

Lou Holtz

"Your patience when you have nothing, and your attitude when you have everything, defines you."

Ashok Sawhney

54

Ego, Pride and Humility

"Have more than thou showest, speak less than thou knowest."

William Shakespeare

"We often refuse to accept an idea merely because the tone of voice in which it has been expressed is, unsympathetic to us."

Friedrich Nietzsche

"When I let go of what I am, I become what I might be."

Lao Tzu

"It was pride that changed angels into devils; it is humility that makes men angels."

Saint Augustine

"It is our own vanity that makes the vanity of others intolerable to us."

Francois de la Rochefoucauld

"There is only one corner of the universe you can be certain of improving, and that's your own self."

Aldous Huxley

"We make a living by what we get. We make a life by what we give."

Winston S. Churchill

"What the world needs is more geniuses with humility, there are so few of us left."

Oscar Levant

"A slip of the foot you may soon recover, but a slip of the tongue you may never get over."

Benjamin Franklin

"Whenever I climb, I am followed by a dog-called 'Ego'."

Friedrich Nietzsche

"When shall I be free? When 'I (ego) shall cease to be'."

Swamy Ram Tirathi

"We are rarely proud when we are alone."

Voltaire

"Never ruin an apology with an excuse."

Benjamin Franklin

"Giving up your worldly possessions is giving a little. It is when you give yourself, your ego is that you truly give."

Ashok Sawhney

55

Anger, Frustration and Bad Temper

"How much more grievous are the consequences of anger than the causes of it."

Marcus Aurelius

"Anyone can become angry - that is easy but to be angry with the right person, to the right degree, at the right time, for the right purpose, and in the right way - this is not easy."

Aristotle

"Anger is the enemy of non-violence, and pride is a monster that swallows it up."

Mahatma Gandhi

"Any dialogue which begins in anger, ends in shame."

Ashok Sawhney

"Anger is one letter away from danger."

Eleanor Roosevelt

"If you lose your temper, you've lost the argument."

Jane Austen

"I have learned through bitter experience the one supreme lesson to conserve my anger, and as heat conserved is transmitted into energy, even so our anger controlled can be transmitted into a power that can move the world."

Mahatma Gandhi

"A smile costs nothing. Anger is so expensive."

Ravi Shanker

"An angry man is akin to a person without vision."

Ashok Sawhney

"If a small thing has the power to make you angry, does that not indicate something about your size?"

Sydney J Harris

"Holding on to anger is like grasping a hot coal with the intent of throwing it at someone else; you are the one who gets burned."

Buddha

"Anger is an acid that can do more harm to the vessel in which it is stored than to anything on which it is poured."

Mark Twain

"Anger and intolerance are the enemies of correct understanding."

Mahatma Gandhi

"You may not be punished for your anger but you will surely be punished by your anger."

Buddha

"Anger and fear are negative energies. Forgiveness is a highly positive energy."

Casey Costello

"The world needs anger. The world often continues to allow evil because it is not angry enough."

Bede Jarret

"Men in rage strike those that wish them best."

William Shakespeare

"If another can easily anger you, it is because you are off balance with yourself."

Scottie Waves

56

Hero, Leader, Genius and Martyr

"Genius is only the power of making continuous efforts."

Elbert Hubbard

"A leader is one who knows the way, goes the way, and shows the way."

John C. Maxwell

"The martyr cannot be dishonored."

Ralph Waldo Emerson

"Leadership is acting when you see the need, without waiting for someone else to suggest it."

Martin Rhodes

"You cannot be a hero without being a coward."

George Bernard Shaw

"You do not lead by hitting people over the head – that's assault, not leadership."

Dwight D. Eisenhower

"Only one man in a thousand is the leader of men – the other 999 follow women."

Groucho Marx

"Every great man is unique."

Ralph Waldo Emerson

"Talent does what it can. Genius does what it must."

Edward George

"Be a hero. Always say, 'I have no fear.'"

Swami Vivekananda

"I suppose leadership at one time meant muscles; but today it means getting along with people."

Mahatma Gandhi

"One crowded hour of glorious life is worth an age without a name."

Thomas Osbert Mordaunt

"Strong towers decay, but great name shall never pass away."

Park Benjamin

"Good leadership consists of showing average people how to do the work of superior people."

John D. Rockefeller

"Do Something. Either lead, follow or get out of the way."

Ted Turner

"He that would govern others, first should be the master of himself."

Philip Massinger

"Anyone who helps someone selflessly, is a hero to me."

Ashok Sawhney

57

Truth and Falsehood

"Truth is the highest virtue, but higher still is truthful living."

Kiratkarni (Gurbani)

"A sour truth is better than a sweet lie."

Shivanand

"Truth is the highest thing that man may keep."

Geoffrey Chaucer

"Man prefers to believe what he prefers to be true."

Francis Bacon

"All great truths begin as blasphemies."

George Bernard Shaw

"Truth is the cry of all, but the game of the few."

George Berkeley

"The greatest friend of truth is time, her greatest enemy is prejudice and her constant companion is humility."

Charles Caleb Colton

"The truth is often unpopular."

Adlai Stevenson

"Today you are you, that is truer than true. There is no one alive who is your than you."

Albert Einstein

"Never take anything for granted."

Benjamin Disraeli

"Repetition does not transform a lie into a truth."

Franklin D. Roosevelt

"Gossip is what some invent the rest enlarge."

Jonathan Swift

"When you betray somebody else, you also betray yourself."

Issac Bashevis Singer

"One must be as humble as the dust before he can discover truth."

Mahatma Gandhi

"Facts are facts and will not disappear on account of your likes."

Pandit Jawaharlal Nehru

"Facts are many, but the truth is one."

Rabindranath Tagore

"Even if you are a minority of one, the truth is the truth."

Mahatma Gandhi

"Three things cannot be long hidden: the sun, the moon, and the truth."

Buddha

"Never tell the truth to people who are not worthy of it."

Mark Twain

"Whenever you have truth it must be given with love, or the message and the messenger will be rejected."

Mahatma Gandhi

"Get your facts first then you can distort them as you please."

Mark Twain

"To be outspoken is easy when you do not wait to speak the complete truth."

Rabindranath Tagore

"If you do not seek the truth by yourself, you will be misled."

Lailah Gifty Akita

"Truth never damages a cause that is just."

Mahatma Gandhi

"No man has a good enough memory to be a successful liar."

Abraham Lincoln

"In all debates, let truth be thy aim, not victory, or an unjust interest."

William Penn

"Where an opinion is general, it is usually correct."

Jane Austen

"Just because you're offended, doesn't mean you're right."

Ricky Gervals

"A rumour can travel several times around the world, while the truth is still putting on slippers."

Ashok Sawhney

58

Time, News and Newspapers

"If you want your children to be good and do well in life, spend double time with them instead of money."

Ashok Sawhney

"The first duty of a newspaper is to be accurate. If it be accurate, it follows that it is fair."

Herbert Bayard Swope

"There was a time when the reader of an unexciting newspaper would remark, 'How dull is the world today!' Nowadays he says, 'What a dull newspaper!'"

Daniel J. Boorstin

"Nowhere else can one find so miscellaneous, so various, an amount of knowledge as is contained in a good newspaper."

Henry Ward Beecher

"Time, which is the author of authors."

Francis Bacon

"To choose time is to save time."

Francis Bacon

"The years teach much which the days never know."

Ralph Waldo Emerson

"Take care of the minutes: for hours will take care of themselves."

Lord Chesterfield

"The great instructor, time."

Edmund Burke

"The inaudible and noiseless foot of time."

William Shakespeare

"There is no waste of time in life, like that of making explanations."

Benjamin Disraeli

"Remember that time is money."

Benjamin Franklin

"When a dog bites a man that is not news, but when a man bites a dog that is news."

Charles Anderson Dane

"Nowadays truth is the greatest news."

Thomas Fuller

"Evil news rides post, while good news baits."

John Milton

"Time is the great physician."

Benjamin Disraeli

"If it's far away, it's news, but if it's close at home, it's sociology."

James Reston

"The time to relax is when you do not have time for it."

Sydney Harris

"No time like the present."

Mary de la Riviere Manley

"No army can withstand the strength of an idea whose time has come."

Victor Hugo

"The best time to memorize anything is just before you go to sleep."

John Lodge

"The two most powerful warriors are patience and time."

Leo Tolstoy

"A man does not have the time to spend half of his life in quarrels."

Dale Carnegie

"True friendship resists time, distance and silence."

Mark Twain

"Can anybody remember when the times were not hard and money not scarce?"

Ralph Waldo Emerson

"Don't wait. The time will never be just right."

Mark Twain

"Don't count the days, make the days count."

Muhammad Ali

"Words are the only things that last forever."

William Hazlitt

"What we love to do, we find time to do."

John L. Spalding

"I had only two difficult times in my whole life, one before you met me, the other after you left me."

Ashok Sawhney

59

Success and Failure, Losing and Winning

"Many of life's failures are experienced by people who did not realize how close they were to success when they gave up."

Thomas Edison

"By failing to prepare, you are preparing to fail."

Benjamin Franklin

"Tempt not a desperate man."

William Shakespeare

"Man can climb to the highest summits, but he cannot dwell there long."

George Bernard Shaw

"Before everything else, getting ready is the secret of success."

Henry Ford

"Success does not consist in never making mistakes but in never making the same one a second time."

George Bernard Shaw

"Success is the ability to go from failure to failure without losing your enthusiasm."

Winston Churchill

"The secret of success is constancy to purpose."

Benjamin Disraeli

"I have not failed. I've just found 10,000 ways that won't work."

Thomas Alva Edison

"A minute's success pays the failure of years."

Robert Browning

"It is easy to fall, but hard to rise."

Dann Moudry

"When I was young, I observed that nine out of ten things I did were failures. So I did ten times more work."

George Bernard Shaw

"The secret of success in conversation is to be able to discharge without being disagreeable."

Bert kelly

"Success is not the key to happiness. Happiness is the key to success. If you love what you are doing, you will be successful."

Herman Cain

"Moderation is a fatal thing. Nothing succeeds like excess."

Oscar Wilde

"A successful man may or may not be happy, but a man who is happy is bound to be successful."

Ashok Sawhney

"I attribute my success to this: I never gave or took any excuse."

Florence Nightingale

"Ambition is the last refuge of the failure."

Oscar Wilde

"Judge your success by what you had to give up in order to get it."

Dalai Lama

"What seems to us as bitter trials are often blessings in disguise."

Oscar Wilde

"The successful warrior is the average man, with laser-like focus."

Bruce Lee

"Before anything else, preparation is the key to success."

Alexander Graham Bell

"The road to success is always under construction."

Lily Tomlin

"Success is the sum of small efforts, repeated day-in and day-out."

Robert Collier

"Patience, persistence and perspiration make an unbeatable combination for success."

Napoleon Hill

"I am thankful for all of those who said no to me. It's because of them I'm doing it myself."

Albert Einstein

"Success will not lower its standard to us. We must raise our standard to success."

Randall McBride

"It is wise to keep in mind that neither success nor failure is ever final."

Roger Babson

"I've failed over and over and over again in my life and that is why I succeed."

Michael Jordan

"Winners never quit, and quitters never win."

Ted Turner

"Defeat is not bitter unless you swallow it."

Joe Clark

"We didn't lose the game; we just ran out of time."

Vince Lombardi

"A successful man is one who can lay a firm foundation with bricks others have thrown at him."

David Brinkley

"Striving for success without hard work is like trying to harvest where you haven't planted."

David Bly

"There's always something about your success that displeases even your best friends."

Mark Twain

"After failing to climb Mountain Everest, Edmund Hillary said: Hey Everest; I will come back again! As a mountain you can't grow, but as a man I can."

Edmund Hillary

"It's better to step back when ignored. Rather than waiting to be insulted."

Vamshi Kurra

"Every adversity, every failure, every heartache carries with it the seed of an equal or greater benefit."

Napoleon Hill

"Success consists of going from failure to failure without loss of enthusiasm."

Winston Churchill

"Our greatest glory is not in never falling but in rising every time we fall."

Confucius

"There is only one thing that makes a dream impossible to achieve: the fear of failure."

Paulo Coelho

"Think twice before you speak, because your words and influence will plant the seed of either success or failure in the mind of another."

Napoleon Hill

"Wherever you see a successful business, someone once made a courageous decision."

Peter Drucker

"When you win, say nothing. When you lose, say less."

Paul Brown

"Strive not to be a success, but rather to be of value."

Albert Einstein

"Success is not final, failure is not fatal: it is the courage to continue that counts."

Winston Churchill

"Success is most often achieved by those who don't know that failure is inevitable."

Coco Chanel

"Success is a journey not a destination."

Ben Sweetland

"When everything seems to be going against you, remember that the airplane takes off against the wind, not with it."

Henry Ford

"You always pass failure on the way to success."

Mickey Rooney

"Success usually comes to those who are too busy to be looking for it."

Henry Thoreau

"Success is getting what you want; happiness is wanting what you get."

Dale Carnegie

"By failing to prepare, you are preparing to fall."

Benjamin Franklin

"Success is how high you bounce when you hit bottom."

George S. Patton

"Asks the Possible to the Impossible, 'Where is your dewelling place?' 'In the dream of the impotent' comes the answer."

Rabindranath Tagore

"Sometimes in the winds of change, we find our true direction."

Robinson Ocean

"The difficult is what takes a little time, the impossible is what takes a little longer."

Fridtjof Nansen

" 'Tis a lesson you should heed: 'There is nothing which we receive with so much reluctance as advice.'"

Joseph Addison

"Unsolicited advice is the cheapest commodity you can find because the supply is so great and the demand so little."

Richard Nixon

"Fall seven times, stand up eight."

Nana Korobi ya Oki

"Every rise has to ultimately fall, and every fall has to rise after all."

Ashok Sawhney

60

Money, Wealth and Price

"When you have money in hand, only you forget who are you. But when you do not have any money in your hand, the whole world forgets who you are. It's life."

Bill Gates

"Security depends not so much upon how much you have, as upon how much you can do without."

Joseph Wood Krutch

"I agree, money isn't God, but believe me, these days, it isn't less than any God."

Ashok Sawhney

"The amount of money that's in your bank at the time of death, is the extra work you did which was not necessary."

Adolph Hitler

"We have no more right to consume happiness without producing it, than to consume wealth without producing it."

George Bernard Shaw

"When a man says money can do anything, that settles it: he hasn't got any."

George Bernard Shaw

"Money – money, like everything else – is a deception and a disappointment."

Herbert George Wells

"Money can't buy happiness but it surely is a source to make life a lot easier."

Ashok Sawhney

"Lack of money is the root of all evil."

George Bernard Shaw

"To be at once exceedingly wealthy and good is impossible."

Plato

"The best way to make money is to not lose any."

Ann Landers

"The best client is a scared millionaire."

H.L. Mencken

"Do what you love and the money will follow."

Marsha Sinetar

"The price of anything is the amount of life you exchange for it."

Henry David Thoreau

"First we sacrifice health to make money, then we sacrifice money to regain lost health."

Dalai Lama

"Too much of everything is bad but you can never have too much money."

Ashok Sawhney

"The most unfortunate part of life is when people want to make money without earning it."

Shiv Khera

"Money does not make you happy but it quitens the nerves."

Sean O'Casey

"Money has power but not truth."

Ashok Sawhney

61

Fate, Luck, Fortune and Destiny

"All fate is dangerous! Good bringeth envy, bad, shame."

Thomas Fuller

"Man is man and master of his fate."

Alfred Lord Tennyson

"There is no armour against fate."

James Shirley

"I find that the harder I work, the more luck I seem to have."

Thomas Jefferson

"A person's fate is their own temper."

Benjamin Disraeli

"Luck is a dividend of sweat. The more you sweat, the luckier you get."

Ray Kroc

"There is no such thing as accident! It is fate misnamed."

Napolean Bonaparte

"Be faithful in small things because it is in them that your strength lies."

Mother Teresa

"Make the best use of what is in your power, and take the rest as it happens."

Epictetus

"Remember that not getting what you want is sometimes a wonderful stroke of luck."

Dalai Lama

"Calamities are of two kinds; misfortunes to ourselves and good fortune to others"

A. Bierce

"Men heap together mistakes of their lives and create a monster they call destiny."

John Oliver Hobbes

"It is choice not chance, that determines your destiny."

Jean Nidetch

"It is health that is real wealth and not pieces of gold and silver."

Mahatma Gandhi

"You are the creator of your own destiny."

Swami Vivekananda

"Control your own destiny or someone else will."

Jack Welch

"Why get your prayers insulted, when you know, everything else can change, but not your destiny."

Ashok Sawhney

62

Stress, Strain and Tension

"The time to relax is when you don't have time for it."

Sydney J. Harris

"You're in pretty good shape for the shape you are in."

Dr. Seuss

"It is not a daily increase, but a daily decrease. Hack away at the inessentials."

Bruce Lee

"The greatest weapon against stress is our ability to choose one thought over another."

William James

"It's not stress that kills us, it is our reaction to it."

Hans Selye

"For fast-acting relief, try slowing down."

Lily Tomlin

"A crust eaten in peace is better than a banquet partaken in anxiety."

Aesop

"Rule number one is, don't sweat the small stuff. Rule number two is, it's all small stuff."

Robert Eliot

"Stressed is desserts spelled backwards."

Carver

"Life is difficult and those who make us laugh are angels."

Wayne Gerard Trotman

"You do not get stomach ulcers from what your eat. You get ulcers from what is eating you."

Dr. Jospeh Montage

"Nothing will make you look old sooner than tension and fatigue."

Dale Carnegie

"What worries you masters you."

Hardon W. Robinson

"Anxiety and distress, interrupted occasionally by pleasure, is the normal course of man's existence."

Joseph Wood Krutch

"Our stress and strain is because of the daily increase of our inessentials."

Ashok Sawhney

63

Miscellaneous

"Statistics show that of those who contract the habit of eating, very few survive."

George Bernard Shaw

"All fingers are not same in length, but when they are bent all stand equal. Life becomes easy when we bend and adjust to situations."

Herryicm

"A precedent embalms a principle."

Benjamin Disraeli

"Quarrels would not last long if the fault was only on one side."

La Rouchefoucauld

"A prisoner cannot liberate other prisoners."

Shivanand

"One with the law is a majority."

Calvin Coolidge

"If you would wish another to keep your secret, first keep it yourself."

Seneca

"Never argue with your doctor – he has inside information."

Ben Brinker

"Celibacy isn't it hereditary."

Carole Marsh

"What is the difference between American and Indian democracies? In America you can kiss in public but not pee. In India, you can pee in public but not kiss."

Manoranjan Kumar

"A wonderful thing about a book, in contrast to a computer screen is that you can take it to bed with you."

Daniel J. Boorstein

"Some men have only one book in them, others, a library."

Sydney Smith

"A bend in the road is not the end of the road, unless you fail to make the turn."

John C. Maxwell

"No question is so difficult to answer as that to which the answer is obvious."

George Bernard Shaw

"The abuse of a thing is no argument against the use of it."

Jeremy Collier

"Continuous improvement is better than delayed perfection."

Mark Twain

"The frontier between hell and heaven is only the difference between two ways of looking at things."

George Bernard Shaw

"A day's life of a lion is better than a hundred years of a jackal."

Tipu Sultan

"Merit is worthier than fame."

Francis Bacon

"What you get free, costs too much."

Jean Anouilh

"A 'no' uttered from the deepest conviction is better than a 'yes' merely uttered to please, or worse, to avoid trouble."

Mahatma Gandhi

"Golf is a good walk spoiled."

Mark Twain

"What is the difference between a taxidermist and a tax collector? The taxidermist takes only your skin."

Mark Twain

"A bad forgery's the ultimate insult."

Jonathan Gash

"No one ever won a game of chess by betting on each move. Sometimes you have to move backward to get a step forward."

Amar Gopal Bose

"Glory is fleeting but obscurity is forever."

Napolean Bonaparte

"Everything comes to us that belongs to us if we create the capacity to receive it."

Rabindranath Tagore

"Accept what you can't change. Change what you can't accept."

Martin Seligman

"Part of the secret of success in life is to eat what you like and let the food fight it out inside."

Mark Twain

"Sometimes things fall apart so that better things can fall together."

Marilyn Monroe

"Flowers don't have a nature to compete with each other, they just bloom."

Ashok Sawhney

"If you are not making mistakes, then you aren't making decisions."

Catherine Cook

"Explore. Dream. Discover."

Mark Twain

"Non-violence does not always work – violence never does."

Madge Michels Cyrus

"I have two doctors, my left leg and my right leg."

G.M. Trovelyon

"Our civil servants are neither civil nor servants."

Winston Churchill

"The worst loneliness is not to be comfortable with yourself."

Mark Twain

"Namaste means the divinity in me salutes the divinity in you."

Srila Prabhupad

"Invention breeds invention."

Ralph Waldo Emerson

"There is a triple sight in blindness keen."

John Keats

"Laws grind the poor, and rich men rule the law."

Oliver Goldsmith

"For a law to be respected, it ought to be worthy of respect. It must be fair and it must be fairly enforced."

Richard Nixon

"Every why hath a wherefore."

William Shakespeare

"I never refuse. I never contradict. I sometimes forget."

Benjamin Disraeli

"There is a charm about the forbidden that makes it unspeakably desirable."

Mark Twain

"There's small choice in rotten apples."

William Shakespeare

"Changed my password everywhere to 'incorrect'. That way when I forget it, it always reminds me 'your password is 'incorrect''."

Steve Carell

"To heal a wound you need to stop touching it."

Jordan Mecale

"Little you get if you complain much, much you get if you complain little."

Ashok Sawhney

64

Rich, Poor, Adversity and Misery

"The rich must live more simply, so that the poor may simply live."

Mahatma Gandhi

"The surest way to remain poor is to be honest."

Napoleon Bonaparte

"Rich bachelors should be heavily taxed. It is not fair that some men should be happier than others."

Oscar Wilde

"Poverty consists in feeling poor."

Ralph Waldo Emerson

"The greatest of evils and the worst of all crime is poverty."

George Bernard Shaw

"If thou wilt make a man happy, add not unto his riches but take away from his desires."

Epicurus

"Sweet are the uses of adversity."

William Shakespeare

"Who, being loved, is poor?"

Oscar Wilde

"Property is organized robbery."

George Bernard Shaw

"A rich man is nothing but a poor man with money."

W.C. Fields

"Very few people can afford to be poor."

George Bernard Shaw

"Loneliness and the feeling of being unwanted is the most terrible poverty."

Mother Teresa

"A poor woman who is not straight is a prostitute, but a rich one is a lady of fashion."

Oscar Wilde

"If you don't think you're rich, try counting all the things you have, that money can't buy."

Rob Hawkins

"You can't comfort the afflicted, without afflicting the comfortable."

Princess Diana of Wales

"Superfluous wealth can buy superfluities only."

Henry David Thoreau

"He that hath nothing is frightened at nothing."

Thomas Fuller

"In prosperity our friends know us; in adversity we know our friends."

John Churton Collins

"The man with a toothache thinks everyone happy whose teeth are sound.
The poverty-stricken man makes the same mistake about the rich man."

George Bernard Shaw

"Quick riches are often more dangerous than poverty."

Napoleon Hill

"A man is rich according to what he is, not according to what he has."

Henry W. Beacher

"Resolve not to be poor: whatever you have, spend less."

Samuel Johnson

"A miser grows rich by seeming poor; an extravagant man grows poor by seeming rich."

William Shenstone

"To be rich, is not what you have in your bank account, but what you have in your heart."

Anonymous

"One should have suffered in poverty, to relish the luxury of giving."

Ashok Sawhney

65

Experience

"Experience is a hard teacher as it gives the test first and the lesson afterwards."

Venom Law

"Knowledge can only be got in one way, the way of experience, there is no other way to know."

Swami Vivekananda

"Forget what hurt you in the past, but never forget what it taught you."

Shanon L. Alder

"Good judgment comes from experience and experience comes from bad judgments."

Bob. Packwood

"Experience is the name men give to their mistakes."

Oscar Wilde

"Experience is not what happens to you, it is what you do with what happens to you."

Aldous Huxley

"It is far better to borrow experience than to buy it."

Charles Caleb Colton

"Learn from the wounds of experience and convert them into wisdom."

Ashok Sawhney

66

Art and Culture

"The aim of art is to represent not the outward appearance of things, but their inward significance."

Aristotle

"You use a glass mirror to see your face; you use works of art to see your soul."

George Bernard Shaw

"A good painter is to paint two main things, men and the working of man's mind."

Leonardo Da Vinci

"The artist wants to show the pain of the birth of a work . . . the pity of it is that all painters are becoming thinkers."

M F Husain

"A picture is a poem without words."

Confucius

"In art, man reveals himself and not his objects."

Rabindranath Tagore

"Art is the elimination of the unnecessary."

Pablo Picasso

"The secret of life is in art."

Oscar Wild

"Art is the child of nature."

Henry Wadsworth Longfellow

"You know who the critics are? The men who have failed in literature and art."

Benjamin Disraeli

"The history of art is the history of revivals."

Samuel Butler

"There is an art of reading, as well as an art of thinking and an art of writing."

Isaac Disraeli

"He who has imagination without learning has wings and no feet."

Joseph Joubert

"Art should never try to be popular."

Oscar Wilde

67

Relationships

"When you educate a man you educate an individual; when you educate a woman you educate a whole family."

R.M. Maciver

"The mother's heart is the child's school room."

Henery Ward Beecher

"As we grew up, my brothers acted like they didn't care, but I always knew they looked out for me and were there for me!"

Catherine Pulsifer

"Sweet is the voice of sister in the season of sorrow."

Benjamin Disraeli

"Make your being so deep and intense that God grants your wishes."

Ashok Sawhney

"A sister smiles when one tells one's stories – for she knows where the decoration has been added."

Chris Montaigne

"Behold, how good and pleasant it is when brothers dwell in unity!"

Psalm

"When nails grow long, we cut nails, not our fingers. Similiarly, when misunderstandings crop up, cut your ego, not relationships."

Anonymous

"All for one; one for all."

Alexander Dumas

"If one friend or a family member is not happy, then their unhappiness can spread to infect others in the group."

Deana Mascle

"All relationships go through hell, real relationships get through it."

Lee Lo

"A great relationship is about appreciating the similarities and respecting the differences."

Jelly Wong

"It takes a second to break relations. But I couldn't do it even after my life's deliberations."

Ashok Sawhney

"The family you come from is not as important as the family you are going to have."

Ring Lardner

"The family is the association established by nature for the supply of man's everyday wants."

Aristotle

"Perhaps the greatest social service that can be rendered by anybody to the country and to mankind is to bring up a family."

George Bernard Shaw

"Our ancestors become invisible forever, much sooner than we would hope them to be."

Ashok Sawhney

68

Need, Greed and Contentment

"Will tell you how to become rich. Close the doors. Be fearful when others are greedy. Be greedy when others are fearful."

Warren Buffett

"Greed is the father of all frauds."

Ashok Sawhney

"Only God can fully satisfy the hungry heart of man."

Hugh Black

"The greatest wealth is to live content with little."

Plato

"He who is not contented with what he has, would not be contented with what he would like to have."

Socrates

"He who is greedy is always insatiable."

Ashok Sawhney

"Selfishness and greed, individual or national, cause most of our troubles."

Harry Truman

"Necessity makes an honest man a knave."

Denial Defoe

"One must be needy and not greedy, the true antidote of greed is contentment."

Ashok Sawhney

69

Patience, Light and Darkness

"Patience, persistence and perspiration make an unbeatable combination for success."

Napoleon Hill

"Patience is the companion of wisdom."

St. Augustine

"When you're tempted to lose patience with someone, think how patient God has been with you all the time."

John Doe

"Words which do not give the light of God increase the darkness."

Mother Teresa

"We can easily forgive a child who is afraid of the dark; the real tragedy of life is when men are afraid of the light."

Plato

"It is during our darkest moments that we must focus to see the light."

Aristotle Onassis

"There is strong shadow where there is much light."

Johann Wolfgang von Goethe

"You must have the light of courage to enlighten those who are in the dark."

Ashok Sawhney

70

Charity and Donation

"A long life may not be good enough, but a good life is long enough."

Benjamin Franklin

"It is the quality of our work which will please God and not the quantity."

Mahatma Gandhi

"Charity is injurious unless it helps the recipient to become independent of it."

John D. Rockefeller

"Charity is a thing that begins at home, and usually stays there."

Elbert Hubbard

"If you haven't got any charity in your heart, you have the worst kind of heart trouble."

Bob Hope

"Not he who has much is rich, but he who gives much."

Erich Fromm

"I learned to give not because I have much, but because I know exactly what it feels like to have nothing."

Diva Fierce

"It isn't how much we give, but how much love we put into giving."

Mother Teresa

"The manner of giving is worth more than the gift."

Pierre Corneille

"When we give cheerfully and accept gratefully, everyone is blessed."

Maya Angelou

"Only by giving, you can sow the seeds for receiving."

Ashok Sawhney

"Speak the truth, do not become angered, and give when asked, even be it a little. By these three conditions one goes to the presence of the Gods."

Gautama Buddha

"It is the apathetic person that sees the cause while the charitable person sees the need."

Shannon L. Alder

"Getters don't get . . . givers get."

Euegene Benge

"Oh, if the good hearts had the fat purses, how much better everything would go!"

Victor Hugo

"The man who leaves money to charity in his will is only giving away what no longer belongs to him."

Voltaire

71

Wit and Humour

"Give me a sense of humor, Lord; give me the grace to see a joke,
To get some happiness from life, and pass it on to other folks."

Dolores Cullen

"Light travels faster than sound. This is why some people appear bright until they speak."

Steve Wright

"If this is coffee please bring me some tea and if this is tea please bring me some coffee."

Abraham Lincoln

"I no doubt deserved my enemies, but I don't believe I deserved my friends."

Walt Whitman

"Originality is the fine art of remembering what you hear but forgetting where you heard it."

Lawrence J. Peter

"Don't take life too seriously. You will never get out of it alive."

Elbert Hubbard

"The golden rule is that there are no golden rules."

George Bernard Shaw

"I feel so miserable without you; it's almost like having you here."

George Bernard Shaw

"The most beautiful words in language: I told you so."

Gore Vidal

"Happiness is having a large, loving, caring, close-knit family in another city."

George Burns

During a meeting, a lady asked Churchill a question. Churchill being a bit hafty, tried to get up, but a smart girl in skirts was faster to get up and reply.
This was repeated again, so G.B. Shaw remarked,
"Eh Churchill, what is happening, this girl in skirts is beating you hollow?
Churchill: Shut up G.B. It is a general rule. When the skirts go up,
The pants go down!!"

"Take my advice, I don't use it anyway."

Geoff Tibballs

"I have no objection to anyone's sex life as long as they don't practice it in the street and frighten the horses."

Oscar Wilde

"I did not attend his funeral, but I sent a nice letter saying I approved of it."

Mark Twain

"I have great faith in fools – self-confidence my friends will call it."

Edgar Allan Poe

"I never thought much of the courage of a lion tamer. Inside the cage he is at least safe from people."

George Bernard Shaw

"Duty is what one expects from others."

Oscar Wilde

"Why do couples hold hands on their wedding day? It's just a formality like boxers shaking hands before a fight."

Junk Crunch

"Her capacity for family affection is extraordinary. When her third husband died, her hair turned quite gold from grief."

Oscar Wilde

"England and America are two countries separated by the same language."

George Bernard Shaw

"I would like to live as a poor man with lots of money."

Pablo Picasso

"I have opinions of my own – but you don't always agree with them."

George W. Bush

"I don't want money. It is only people who pay their bills who want that, and I never pay mine."

Oscar Wilde

"Dancing is a perpendicular expression of a horizontal desire."

George Bernard Shaw

"I am everywhere and I am nowhere. That's the beauty of the internet age."

Ai Weiwei

"If there was nothing wrong in the world there wouldn't be anything for us to do."

George Bernard Shaw

"When I told my doctor I couldn't afford an operation – he offered to touch up my x-rays."

Henny Youngman

"Serious sport has nothing to do with fair play."

George Bernard Shaw

"Why won't sharks attack lawyers? Professional courtesy!"

Gene Helfman

"A gentleman is a patient wolf."

Lana Turner

"Humor is mankind's greatest blessing."

Mark Twain

"Wit is educated insolence."

Aristotle

"Wit and humor belong to genius alone."

Miguel De Cervantes

"There is nothing in the world so irresistibly contagious as laughter and good humor."

Charles Dickens

"Which painting in the National Gallery would I save if there was a fire? The one nearest the door of course."

George Bernard Shaw

"A little sincerity is a dangerous thing, and a great deal of it is absolutely fatal."

Oscar Wilde

"Find enough clever things to say, and you're a Prime Minister; write them down and you're a Shakespeare."

George Bernard Shaw

"I refuse to answer that question on the grounds that I don't know the answer."

Douglas Adams

"Wit beyond measure is man's greatest treasure."

J.K. Rowling

"Women give to men the very gold of their lives. But they invariably want it back in small change."

Oscar Wilde

"Few people think more than two or three times a year; I have made an international reputation for myself by thinking once or twice a week."

George Bernard Shaw

"I have only made this letter longer because I have not had the time to make it shorter."

Blaise Pascal

"A successful book is not made of what is in it, but what is left out of it."

Mark Twain

"Do not do unto others as you expect they should do unto you. Their tastes may not be the same."

George Bernard Shaw

"Everybody who is incapable of learning has taken to teaching."

Oscar Wilde

"If Christ were here there is one thing he would not be – a Christian."

Mark Twain

"A gentleman is one who never hurts anyone's feelings unintentionally."

Oscar Wilde

"Nothing spoils a romance so much as a sense of humour in the woman – or the want of it in the man."

Oscar Wilde

"If you leave the smallest corner of your head vacant for a moment, other people's opinions will rush in from all quarters."

George Bernard Shaw

"There is no greater hiding place for a secret than within the mind of a madman."

Alexander Ferrick

"Sometimes you can't agree with people because you would both be wrong."

Shannon L. Alder

"If you have to explain your sense of humor, then you are performing for the wrong crowd."

Shannon L. Alder

"Today I am amused, and I haven't seen anyone yet."

Aleksandra Ninkovic

"Cheap editions of great books may be delightful, but cheap editions of great men are absolutely detestable."

Oscar Wilde

"I never resist temptation, because I have found that things that are bad for me do not tempt me."

George Bernard shaw

"The difference between your crazy and my crazy is that you don't think you're crazy."

Steve Maraboli

"Think of what makes you smile; makes you happy . . . and do more of that shit."

Steve Maraboli

"'Jimmy Murray, you are an ass,' said Aunt Ruth, angrily.
'Well, we're cousins,' agreed cousin Jimmy pleasantly."

L.M. Montgomery

"Nobody ever goes to that store to shop because it's too crowded."

Sol Luckman

"If you've brains it's better than beauty – brains last, beauty doesn't."

L.M. Montgomery

"Why should we take advice on sex from the pope? If he knows anything about it, he shouldn't!"

George Bernard Shaw

"I wish for you the wisdom to mind your own business."

Steve Maraboli

"There is only one thing in life worse than being talked about, and that is not being talked about."

Oscar Wilde

"My doctor says I must not have any serious conversation after seven [o'clock]. It makes me talk in my sleep."

Oscar Wilde

"The problem is, God gave man a brain and a penis and only enough blood to run one at a time."

Robin McLaurin Williams

"As long as a woman can look ten years younger than her daughter, she is perfectly satisfied."

Oscar Wilde

"One advantage of talking to yourself is that you know at least somebody's listening."

Franklin P. Jones

"If one tells the truth, one is sure, sooner or later, to be found out."

Oscar Wilde

"Better a witty fool than a foolish wit."

William Shakespeare

"Brevity is the soul of wit."

William Shakespeare

"If you can't get a compliment any other way, pay yourself one."

Mark Twain

"I am so clever that sometimes I don't understand a single word of what I am saying."

Oscar Wilde

"If stupidity got us into this mess, then why can't it get us out?"

Will Rogers

"Show me a sane man and I will cure him for you."

C.G. Jung

"I like men who have a future and women who have a past."

Oscar Wilde

"If I were two-faced, would I be wearing this one?"

Abraham Lincoln

"Few things are harder to put up with than a good example."

Mark Twain

"The only way to get rid of a temptation is to yield to it."

Oscar Wilde

"My own business always bores me to death; I prefer other people's."

Oscar Wilde

"You can get anything you want at Alice's Restaurant (except Alice)."

Arlo Guthrie

"He has all of the virtues I dislike and none of the vices I admire."

Winston Churchill (On Sir Richard Stafford Cripps)

"As I get older I notice the years less and the seasons more."

John Hubbard

"Happiness is good health and a bad memory."

Ingrid Bergman

"Men are like steel; when they lose their temper, they lose their worth."

Chuck Norris

"Copy from one, it's plagiarism; copy from two, it's research."

Wilson Mizner

"When I was young, I thought without money life would be miserable. Now being old I know that it is."

Ashok Sawhney

"If you owe the bank $100 that's your problem. If you owe the bank $100 million, that's the bank's problem."

J. Paul Getty

"A woman worries about her future till she gets a husband. A man never worries about his future until he gets a wife."

Charles M. Schwab

"Marriage is a book of which the first chapter is written in poetry and the remaining chapters written in prose."

Beverly Nichols

"When I was called upon to be Prime Minister, now nearly two years ago, there were not many applicants for the job. Since then perhaps the market has improved."

Winston Churchill

"You cheat me once, it is a shame on you, you cheat me twice, it is a shame on me."

Shad Helmsteter

"The older I grow, the more I distrust the familiar doctrine that age brings wisdom."

H.L. Mencken

"True friends stab you in the front."

Oscar Wilde

"Age is something that doesn't matter, unless you are a cheese."

Luis Bunuel

"All I can say is that I have taken more out of alcohol than alcohol has taken out of me."

Winston Churchill

"I saw few die of hunger; of overeating a hundred thousands."

Benjamin Franklin

"All women become like their mothers. That is their tragedy. No man does. That's his."

Oscar Wilde

"Women do not lie about their age. In fact, no woman ever has, it's just that memory is the first thing to go."

David C. Holley

"When I was younger I made it a rule never to take strong drink before lunch. It is now my rule never to do so before breakfast."

Winston Churchill

"St. Francis Xavier went to Goa and said, 'Jesus rose from the dead.' Nobody bothered or cared. He then said, 'Jesus turned water into wine.'
Most of Goa converted to Christianity."

Sita Ram Goel

"A minister of finance is a legally authorized pickpocket."

Paul Revere

"Good humor is one of the best articles of dress one can wear in society."

William Thackeray

"Wine is a constant proof that God loves us and loves to see us happy."

Benjamin Franklin

"Wit makes its own welcome and levels all distinctions."

Ralph Waldo Emerson

"A thing well said will be wit in all languages."

John Dryden

"Wit is the salt of converstion, not the food."

William Hazlitt

"Everyday, thousands of innocent plants are killed by vegetarians. Help end the violence."

Anonymous

"It is good thing for an uneducated to read books of quotations."

Winston Churchill

"The day you lose your sense of humour and stop laughing, is the day you grow old."

Ashok Sawhney

72

Global Proverbs

"The genius, unit, and spirit of a Nation are discovered in its proverbs."

Francis Bacon

"Proverbs contain the distilled wisdom of all ages."

Parmod Batra

"A proverb is the wisdom of many but the wit of one."

Lord John Russel

"The same boiling water that hardens the egg, will soften the potato. It all depends upon individual's reaction to stressful circumstances."

English Proverb

"When eating fruit, think of the person who planted the tree."

Vietnamese Proverb

"Habits are first cobwebs, then cables."

Spanish Proverb

"No road is long with good company."

Turkish Proverb

"A tree must love the ground on which it sands."

Russian Proverb

"Vows made in storms are forgot in calms."

English Proverb

"Conscience betrays guilt."

Latin Proverb

"Tell me, I forget. Show me, I remember. Involve me, I understand."

Chinese Proverb

"The wise inherit honor but fools get only shame."

Swiss Proverb

"Conscience is the voice of the soul."

Polish Proverb

"A wise man never knows all. Only fools know everything."

German Proverb

"Intelligence is in the head, not in the age."

Azerbaijani Proverb

"What soap is to the body, laughter is to the soul."

Yiddish Proverb

"Hunger is the best sauce."

Mexican Proverb

"Better to light a candle than to curse the darkness."

Chinese Proverb

"Gold can never be pure and men can never be perfect."

Chinese proverb

"To know road ahead, ask those coming back."

Chinese Proverb

"A smooth sea never made a skilled sailor."

English Proverb

"The hands that serve are holier than lips that pray."

English Proverb

"If you are bitter at heart, sugar in the mouth will not help."

Jewish Proverb

"If you are patient in one moment of anger, you will escape a hundred days of sorrow."

Chinese Proverb

"Give a man a fish, and he'll eat for a day. Teach him how to fish and he'll eat forever."

Chinese Proverb

"An army of sheep lead by a lion, can defeat an army of lions lead by a sheep."

Chinese Proverb

"I don't ask for a lighter burden, but for broader shoulders."

Jewish Proverb

"If the teacher be corrupt, the world will be corrupt."

Persian Proverb

"A bad word whispered will echo a hundred miles."

Chinese Proverb

"It is better to see something once, than to hear about it a thousand times."

Asian Proverb

"When don't have what we like, we must like, what we have."

French Proverb

"You may find the worst enemy or best friend in yourself."

English Proverb

"He who would eat the nut, must first crack the shell."

English Proverb

"When you are born, you cry, and the world rejoices. When you die, you should rejoice, while the world cries."

Indian Proverb

"It is better is have an empty pocket than having an empty mind."

German Proverb

"The axe forgets but the tree remembers."

African Proverb

"May we exist like the lotus at ease in muddy water."

Zen Proverb

"Grass does not grow faster, if you pull on it."

African Proverb

"For the beauty of the rose we also water the thorns."

African Proverb

PROVERBS WITH MEANING:

1. "Keep your friends close and your enemies closer."
   (If you have an enemy, pretend to be friends with them instead of openly fighting with them. That way you can watch them carefully and figure out what they're planning.)
2. "A picture is worth a thousand words."
   (Pictures convey emotions and messages better than written or spoken explanations.)
3. "There's no such thing as a free lunch."
   (Things that are offered for free always have a hidden cost.)
4. "The early bird catches the worm."
   (You should wake up and start work early if you want to succeed.)
5. "Actions speak louder than words."
   (Just saying that you'll do something doesn't mean much. Actually doing it is harder and more meaningful.)
6. "If you can't beat 'em, join 'em."
   (When you try to change someone's behavior and it doesn't work, you might have to change instead. For example, if you're trying to get your classmates to focus on studying but they want to party, maybe you should just party with them.)
7. "One man's trash is another man's treasure."
   (Different people have different ideas about what's valuable.)
8. "Good things come to those who wait."
   (Be patient. Eventually something good will happen to you.)
9. "Two heads are better than one."
   (When two people cooperate with each other, they come up with better ideas.)
10. "The grass is always greener on the other side of the hill."
    (People tend to want whatever they don't have.)
11. "Do unto others as you would have them do unto you."
    (Treat others as you want to be treated.)

12. "A chain is only as strong as its weakest link."
    (If one member of a team doesn't perform well, the whole team will fail.)
13. "Honesty is the best policy."
    (Don't lie.)
14. "Absence makes the heart grow fonder."
    (Sometimes it's good to be away from your partner, because it makes you want to see each other again.)
15. "You can lead a horse to water, but you can't make him drink."
    (If you try to help someone, but they don't take your advice or offers, give up. You can't force someone to accept your help.)
16. "Don't count your chickens before they hatch."
    (Your plans might not work out, so don't start thinking about what you'll do after you succeed. Wait until you've already succeeded, and then you can think about what to do next.)
17. "If you want something done right, you have to do it yourself."
    (Don't trust other people to do important things for you. You have to do things yourself to control the quality of the results.)

PROVERBS ON ROAD SAFETY AND SOME SIGN BOARDS:

1. Hurry will give you worry.
2. Be gentle on my curves.
3. I am curvaceous, be sober.
4. If you are married, divorce speed.
5. Feel my curves, don't test them.
6. Go by sight not by faith.
7. Take your time, not your life.
8. Speed thrills, but kills.
9. If you drink, don't drive. If you drive, don't drink.
10. Don't jump the red light.

Other Books by the Author

KHUSHBOO-E-CHAMAN
(A collection of Urdu poetry)

SURBHI SUMAN
(A book of Urdu poetry in Hindi)

KYA KYUN KAISE
(Answers to questions based on rituals and religious practices)

WHY
(Answers to questions that have always baffled you)

(Available on all leading book stores pan India and also on Amazon)